AMERICA
Sails the Seas

by J. O'H. COSGRAVE II

1 9 6 2

HOUGHTON MIFFLIN COMPANY BOSTON

The Riverside Press Cambridge

This book
is dedicated to the late
CHARLES H. HALL
an editor of
Yachting
and a helpful friend
to all ship lovers.

Chesapeake Dugout　　　　　　*Seminole Dugout*

WHEN WE THINK about the ships that made America it is like walking down a long road. The beginning steps are lost in the past, the present very clear and the future unknown.

　The first known American vessels were described by early explorers who visited Chesapeake Bay. These craft were dugouts, blunt-ended, hollowed from large logs by burning a little bit at a time and removing the charred wood with a sea shell or crude stone tools. They were poled in shallow water and paddled in deeper areas. An improved version of this craft is the Seminole dugout. The lines are finer and the ends sharp, making the craft easier to propel.

　Along the inland waters on the southern part of the Pacific Coast the tule grass or marsh reeds grow abundantly. Here the coastal Indians tied the reeds with rope plaited from rushes into three or four long bundles which they joined into a crude raft very much like the boats made by the Egyptians in 6000 B.C. Out on the Great Plains, where neither bark nor large logs were to be found, the Gros Ventre Indians used "bullboats" made of buffalo skins sewn together and stretched over a circular frame of saplings.

3

Southwest Coast Tule Raft　　　*Missouri River Bullboats*

Haida Indian Dugout Canoes

On the northwest Pacific Coast where the inlets are deep and the densely wooded mountains come down into the sea, the yellow cedar grows to huge size, making it possible to build large dugout canoes. Some of these open, round-bottomed vessels were 60 feet long. Their long sharp overhanging bows and flaring sides were decorated and carved with tribal totems for good luck. These seaworthy canoes were used by the Haida Indians as their chief means of transportation, for fishing and for whaling.

In the well-forested areas of America the Indians developed a canoe that was extraordinary for its lightness and utility. To make this craft, they placed on a level area a piece of birch bark the full size of the canoe. Putting rocks upon this in the general pattern of the bottom, they bent the sides up and held them in place by stakes in the ground.

4

Penobscot Canoe   *Chippewa Canoe*

Around the edge a shaped rail was lashed to the bark with split-spruce-root lacings. They lined the inside of the canoe with very thin strips of cedar running the full length, and reinforced it with ribs of thin green cedar set close together. When the hull was complete it was made watertight with pitch. The overhanging bow and flaring sides were decorated with tribal totems for good luck.

Almost every major Indian tribe had a different type of canoe, depending on the locality and uses. On open rivers and lakes where there were no overhanging trees, the canoes had high bows and sterns. This made the vessel more seaworthy and also made it possible for the Indians to use the canoes, turned over on shore, as shelters at night.

The good lines, lightness, and seaworthiness of these Indian designs were adopted by the French in building larger canoes that were used for exploration and trade all over the Great Lakes and Mississippi Valley areas.

The Hudson's Bay Company used even larger versions of these canoes to supply their far-flung outposts with trade goods and to carry back to civilization the furs brought into the posts from the surrounding wilderness.

5

Hudson's Bay Canoe

According to Norse sagas and songs, Leif Ericsson while on a voyage from Norway to Greenland in A.D. 1000 was blown off course. Carried before an easterly gale, he missed Greenland and accidentally reached North America. The site of the landing called "Vineland" has never been positively identified. It could have been Labrador or possibly farther south. Later sagas tell of other Norsemen who reached North America. Fortunately, we know what their ships were like from discoveries made in burial mounds found in Norway. The Norsemen had the custom of burying their chiefs in their boats surrounded by all their equipment; and at Oseberg and Gokstad the burial mounds were made of blue clay, which protected and preserved everything until the sites were excavated.

The typical vessel was a large double-ended open boat from 70 to 80 feet long, with a 16-foot beam, and 6 feet from keel to rail amidships. It was built of oak with a heavy external keel and a high stem and stern post. The mast could be raised to carry a square sail or lowered

6

Cutaway of a Viking Ship or Drakkar

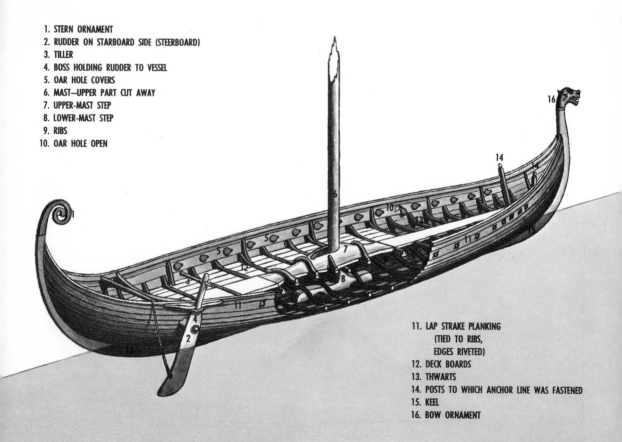

1. STERN ORNAMENT
2. RUDDER ON STARBOARD SIDE (STEERBOARD)
3. TILLER
4. BOSS HOLDING RUDDER TO VESSEL
5. OAR HOLE COVERS
6. MAST—UPPER PART CUT AWAY
7. UPPER-MAST STEP
8. LOWER-MAST STEP
9. RIBS
10. OAR HOLE OPEN

11. LAP STRAKE PLANKING
    (TIED TO RIBS,
    EDGES RIVETED)
12. DECK BOARDS
13. THWARTS
14. POSTS TO WHICH ANCHOR LINE WAS FASTENED
15. KEEL
16. BOW ORNAMENT

Viking Drakkar, A.D. 1000

when the ship was being rowed. The oars, from 12 to 16 to a side, were
handled by oarsmen seated on the crosswise thwarts, under which each
oarsman had a chest for his weapons and eating utensils. When under
sail the oars were unshipped and laid on the thwarts. Wooden lids
sealed the oar holes and the rowers placed their shields over the covers
along the rail as a further protection against wind and spray. The tent
over the midship section sheltered the men off duty and made a place
for them to sleep in their leather sleeping bags. There was no pro-
vision for cooking at sea. Dried meat, dried bread, nuts, and meal
mixed with fat were washed down with water or mead.

Small boats very similar to the Viking ships are still in use in
Scandinavian countries and in Scotland. The familiar whaleboat is the
direct descendant of these most seaworthy of all early vessels. 7

The SANTA MARIA

Among all the ships that made American history the most widely known are those of Christopher Columbus. Unfortunately, there are no plans, drawings, or dimensions of any of the great explorer's vessels made by his contemporaries. Nevertheless, we are certain about the sail plan, for Columbus described it in his journals. The three shown here are typical ships of the period scaled to the approximate sizes of the *Pinta, Niña,* and *Santa Maria.* Contrary to the general opinion, these ships were sound weatherly vessels and, for their time, capable of fast sailing.

There was nothing luxurious about an ocean voyage on a ship of this era. The men rolled up in a blanket on a "soft plank" anywhere they could find a clear space to sleep. The food was cooked in a small

The NIÑA and the PINTA

sandbox called the fourgon, which had a high back to keep the char-
coal fire under the iron and pottery cooking utensils from blowing
away. Victuals were simple — dried bread and garlic for breakfast, salt
meat stewed or fried for dinner, served with water and wine.

Columbus had a cabin to himself, while his officers had smaller
cabins on the main deck. Whatever washing there was took place
in a bucket, since water was a very scarce commodity on board.
Toilet facilities consisted of a board to sit on projecting over the
lee side of the ship: one for the officers, and one for the crew.
Food slops and garbage were sometimes dropped into the bilge.
As a result vermin were plentiful and the stench of the bilge
dreadful.

9

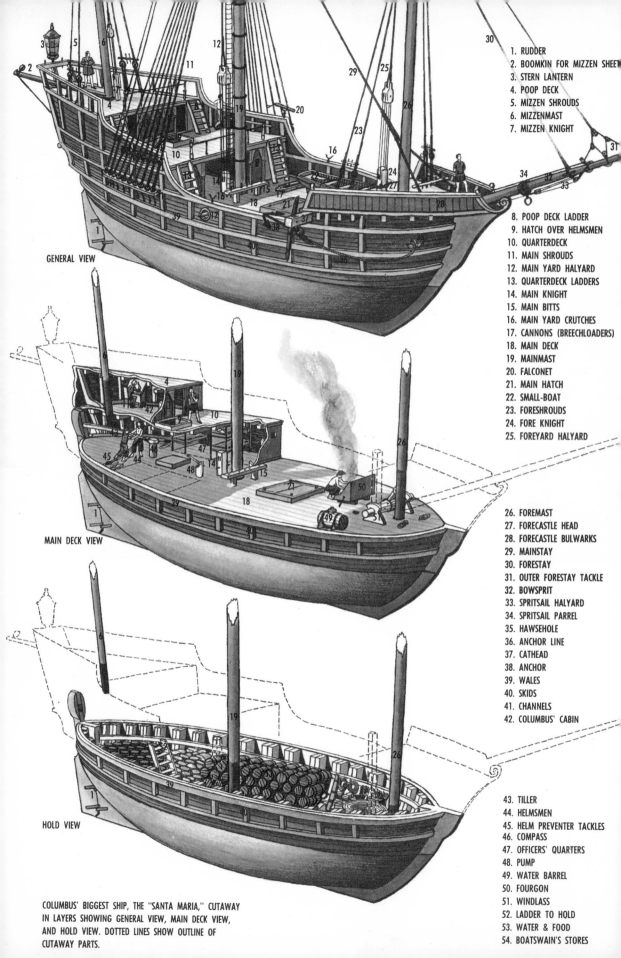

GENERAL VIEW

MAIN DECK VIEW

HOLD VIEW

1. RUDDER
2. BOOMKIN FOR MIZZEN SHEET
3. STERN LANTERN
4. POOP DECK
5. MIZZEN SHROUDS
6. MIZZENMAST
7. MIZZEN KNIGHT

8. POOP DECK LADDER
9. HATCH OVER HELMSMEN
10. QUARTERDECK
11. MAIN SHROUDS
12. MAIN YARD HALYARD
13. QUARTERDECK LADDERS
14. MAIN KNIGHT
15. MAIN BITTS
16. MAIN YARD CRUTCHES
17. CANNONS (BREECHLOADERS)
18. MAIN DECK
19. MAINMAST
20. FALCONET
21. MAIN HATCH
22. SMALL-BOAT
23. FORESHROUDS
24. FORE KNIGHT
25. FOREYARD HALYARD

26. FOREMAST
27. FORECASTLE HEAD
28. FORECASTLE BULWARKS
29. MAINSTAY
30. FORESTAY
31. OUTER FORESTAY TACKLE
32. BOWSPRIT
33. SPRITSAIL HALYARD
34. SPRITSAIL PARREL
35. HAWSEHOLE
36. ANCHOR LINE
37. CATHEAD
38. ANCHOR
39. WALES
40. SKIDS
41. CHANNELS
42. COLUMBUS' CABIN

43. TILLER
44. HELMSMEN
45. HELM PREVENTER TACKLES
46. COMPASS
47. OFFICERS' QUARTERS
48. PUMP
49. WATER BARREL
50. FOURGON
51. WINDLASS
52. LADDER TO HOLD
53. WATER & FOOD
54. BOATSWAIN'S STORES

COLUMBUS' BIGGEST SHIP, THE "SANTA MARIA," CUTAWAY
IN LAYERS SHOWING GENERAL VIEW, MAIN DECK VIEW,
AND HOLD VIEW. DOTTED LINES SHOW OUTLINE OF
CUTAWAY PARTS.

Fishing Vessels off Newfoundland, 15th Century

For at least fifty years before 1492, the fishermen of Spain, Portugal, and Brittany had been sailing to the Newfoundland banks, catching fish and going ashore on Newfoundland to salt and dry them. But fishermen are notoriously uncommunicative. They are not explorers, map makers, or historians. They go to sea to catch fish and are not prone to tell where they get them.

However, a chart, made in 1424 by the Venetian cartographer Zuane Pizzigano, based on information brought to him by Portuguese explorers, shows land beyond the Azores called Antilia that might be North America and land to the north called Satanazes that could be Greenland.

It detracts nothing from Columbus to say that other men were on America's shores before he was. Columbus was important because he opened up the New World. He showed how to go, how to return, and how to colonize.

11

The DAUPHINE on Narragansett Bay, 1524

Today when mariners sail the seas, they have accurate charts showing all the perils of rocks and shoals. Imagine how hazardous a voyage was before there were charts, buoys, and lighthouses. A seaman's sixth sense and a great deal of luck went with these early explorers.

Giovanni da Verrazano had both seaman's sixth sense and luck. After having captured two of Cortez' treasure ships for Francis I of France he was sent by that monarch on a voyage of exploration to claim land for France. His landfall was probably on the coast of North Carolina. From there he worked his way north, navigating by day and anchoring at night. In April, 1524, he discovered Manhattan Island, which he called Angoulême. He sailed past Long Island and into Narragansett Bay, which he named Refugio (Refuge). Here at the mouth of the Taunton River, he traded with the Indians and went ashore at the Indian village of Pakonaket. After sailing around Cape Cod and past Maine, he returned to France, where he wrote an account of his voyage in which he voiced the suspicion that America was 12 a separate continent and not a part of Asia.

After Magellan, Francis Drake was the second man and the first Englishman to sail around the world. He left Plymouth, England, on December 13, 1577, with five ships and 155 men. Two of his ships were found unseaworthy off the Río de la Plata and were set adrift. He sailed through the Strait of Magellan, where one of his ships foundered with all hands and another turned back for England. Drake, in the *Pelican,* made his way up the Pacific Coast of South America, capturing ships, looting towns, and gathering enough booty to make every man aboard rich for life. When the Spaniards set out to chase him, Drake sailed north to California, looking for a secluded spot to beach his ship for repairs. This he found at Drake's Bay, 29 miles north of San Francisco Bay, which he had missed in the fog. A bronze plaque allegedly left by Drake was found in 1936, on the cliffs above Drake's Bay.

From here he sailed across the Pacific, around the Cape of Good Hope, and back to England. The voyage took two years and ten months. When he returned, his ship loaded with captured loot, he was knighted by Queen Elizabeth I. The name of the ship was changed from *Pelican* to *Golden Hind* — perhaps because of her cargo.   13

The PELICAN Careened at Drake's Bay, California, 1579

GODSPEED, DISCOVERY, and SUSAN CONSTANT on Chesapeake Bay, 160?

From Blackwall below London on the Thames, three small ships set out on December 19, 1606, for America. They were the ex-merchantman *Susan Constant,* 74 feet long, *Godspeed,* 45 feet long, and the *Discovery,* 36 feet long. For three weeks the ships were held up at the Downs by unfavorable winds and bad weather. Sailing under the command of Captain Christopher Newport, they stopped at the Azores and the Canary Islands for wood and water. After a rugged crossing of the Atlantic during which very little cooking could be done in the small storm-tossed ships, the weary passengers went ashore at the West Indian island of Nevis to rest and forget the hardships of the voyage.

One hundred and twenty seven days out of London, they entered Chesapeake Bay, anchoring off a point they named Point Comfort. They made charts of the lower part of the James River and explored Jamestown Island, now a peninsula. Sixteen of the colonists had died at sea. The remaining 105 founded the first permanent English settlement in America on May 13, 1607.

14

Henry Hudson, the English explorer employed by the Dutch East Indies Company, was the first navigator to realize the commercial possibilities of New York. He left Amsterdam in Holland on April 4, 1609, sailing north trying to find a passage to the Indies by way of the Arctic Ocean. Difficulties with a troublesome crew forced him to turn back off Novaya Zemlya and head west. He sailed past Newfoundland, stopped at the mouth of the Kennebec River to repair his masts and rigging, then proceeded as far south as Chesapeake Bay. Turning back, he entered New York Bay on September 2, and sailed up the river later named after him. Upon discovering beyond a doubt that the Hudson was not a passage to the sea, he returned, meanwhile surveying the country and making friends with the Indians. On his last voyage in 1611, while still seeking a passage to the Indies, he was set adrift in Hudson's Bay by a mutinous crew. Here he died of exposure.   15

The HALF MOON on the Hudson River, 1609

Although New York had been discovered by Verrazano eighty-five years earlier, no trading had taken place until Hudson's descriptions and surveys showed the commercial potentialities of this rich harbor.

In 1613, two small Dutch vessels entered the harbor of New York. The *Tiger,* commanded by Adriaen Block, and the *Fortyn,* commanded by Captain Hendrick Christiaensen, were loaded with articles suitable for barter with the Indians. The *Fortyn* sailed up the Hudson River to the site of present day Albany where Fort Nassau the first Dutch trading post in America was founded. The *Tiger* anchored off New York, caught fire and burned. Block and his crew salvaged as much of her gear as they could and constructed a new ship near a creek where Broad Street is today. This first ship built in the region was named *Onrust* (meaning restless), 44 feet in length, 11½ feet in beam, and of 16 tons burden. Block sailed her as far north as Cape Cod Bay, making charts as he went. On the basis of his explorations, a charter was granted to the United New Netherland Company for a colony to be called New Netherland.

16

The ONRUST on Buzzards Bay, 1613

The MAYFLOWER

The *Mayflower,* an old, nearly worn-out merchant ship, left Plymouth England on September 6, 1620. On November 9, sixty-four days later, she anchored in Provincetown harbor at the tip of Cape Cod. The crossing for the 102 passengers and the crew of 30 in a ship 90 feet long, beating against westerly gales, was full of the usual maritime hardships of the time. For sanitary accommodation they used buckets; there was very little fresh water for washing, no heat for drying clothes, inadequate ventilation, stale food, and very stale beer. As soon as the anchor was down there arose an understandable clamor to get ashore. There was talk too among the indentured men of breaking away from the colonists entirely. To prevent this and to maintain law and order, the leaders drafted a contract forming them all into a unified group.

Five weeks were spent at Provincetown Bay, where much confusion ensued because the longboat was too small to ferry everyone to shore at once and to carry firewood and water out to the ship. The shallop that was to be used to explore the coast for a suitable spot for the plantation had been stowed in the hold; she was so badly warped that it took the ship's carpenter three weeks to make her seaworthy. In this boat the exploring party sailed along Cape Cod Bay. 17

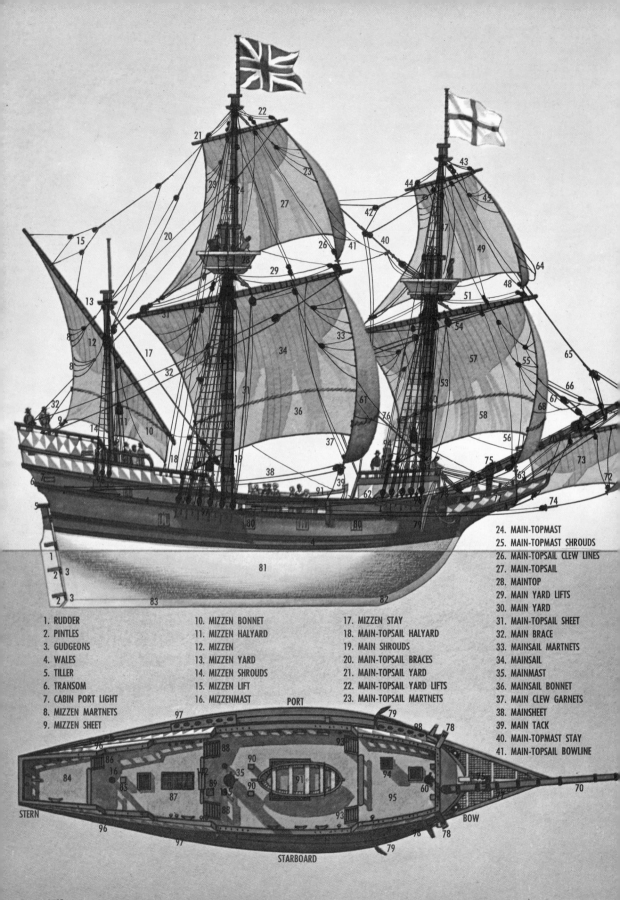

24. MAIN-TOPMAST
25. MAIN-TOPMAST SHROUDS
26. MAIN-TOPSAIL CLEW LINES
27. MAIN-TOPSAIL
28. MAINTOP
29. MAIN YARD LIFTS
30. MAIN YARD
31. MAIN-TOPSAIL SHEET
32. MAIN BRACE
33. MAINSAIL MARTNETS
34. MAINSAIL
35. MAINMAST
36. MAINSAIL BONNET
37. MAIN CLEW GARNETS
38. MAINSHEET
39. MAIN TACK
40. MAIN-TOPMAST STAY
41. MAIN-TOPSAIL BOWLINE

1. RUDDER
2. PINTLES
3. GUDGEONS
4. WALES
5. TILLER
6. TRANSOM
7. CABIN PORT LIGHT
8. MIZZEN MARTNETS
9. MIZZEN SHEET
10. MIZZEN BONNET
11. MIZZEN HALYARD
12. MIZZEN
13. MIZZEN YARD
14. MIZZEN SHROUDS
15. MIZZEN LIFT
16. MIZZENMAST
17. MIZZEN STAY
18. MAIN-TOPSAIL HALYARD
19. MAIN SHROUDS
20. MAIN-TOPSAIL BRACES
21. MAIN-TOPSAIL YARD
22. MAIN-TOPSAIL YARD LIFTS
23. MAIN-TOPSAIL MARTNETS

PORT

STERN

STARBOARD

BOW

The MAYFLOWER—Side and Plan Views

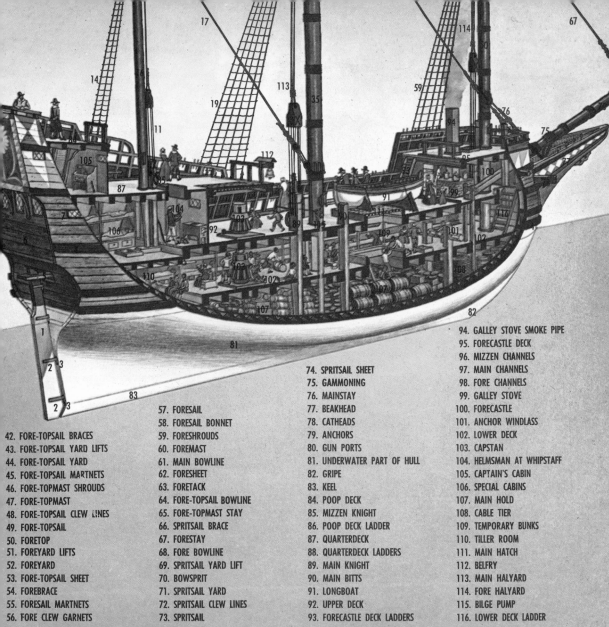

94. GALLEY STOVE SMOKE PIPE
95. FORECASTLE DECK
96. MIZZEN CHANNELS
97. MAIN CHANNELS
98. FORE CHANNELS
99. GALLEY STOVE
100. FORECASTLE
101. ANCHOR WINDLASS
102. LOWER DECK
103. CAPSTAN
104. HELMSMAN AT WHIPSTAFF
105. CAPTAIN'S CABIN
106. SPECIAL CABINS
107. MAIN HOLD
108. CABLE TIER
109. TEMPORARY BUNKS
110. TILLER ROOM
111. MAIN HATCH
112. BELFRY
113. MAIN HALYARD
114. FORE HALYARD
115. BILGE PUMP
116. LOWER DECK LADDER

74. SPRITSAIL SHEET
75. GAMMONING
76. MAINSTAY
77. BEAKHEAD
78. CATHEADS
79. ANCHORS
80. GUN PORTS
81. UNDERWATER PART OF HULL
82. GRIPE
83. KEEL
84. POOP DECK
85. MIZZEN KNIGHT
86. POOP DECK LADDER
87. QUARTERDECK
88. QUARTERDECK LADDERS
89. MAIN KNIGHT
90. MAIN BITTS
91. LONGBOAT
92. UPPER DECK
93. FORECASTLE DECK LADDERS

57. FORESAIL
58. FORESAIL BONNET
59. FORESHROUDS
60. FOREMAST
61. MAIN BOWLINE
62. FORESHEET
63. FORETACK
64. FORE-TOPSAIL BOWLINE
65. FORE-TOPMAST STAY
66. SPRITSAIL BRACE
67. FORESTAY
68. FORE BOWLINE
69. SPRITSAIL YARD LIFT
70. BOWSPRIT
71. SPRITSAIL YARD
72. SPRITSAIL CLEW LINES
73. SPRITSAIL

42. FORE-TOPSAIL BRACES
43. FORE-TOPSAIL YARD LIFTS
44. FORE-TOPSAIL YARD
45. FORE-TOPSAIL MARTNETS
46. FORE-TOPMAST SHROUDS
47. FORE-TOPMAST
48. FORE-TOPSAIL CLEW LINES
49. FORE-TOPSAIL
50. FORETOP
51. FOREYARD LIFTS
52. FOREYARD
53. FORE-TOPSAIL SHEET
54. FOREBRACE
55. FORESAIL MARTNETS
56. FORE CLEW GARNETS

Cutaway of the MAYFLOWER

On December 18, they were forced into Plymouth Harbor by a gale. After two days of exploration, the party returned to the *Mayflower* with the news that they had found a place, and on December 26, the *Mayflower* anchored in Plymouth Harbor.

Here she remained for nearly five months, being used as a barracks for the colonists until buildings could be constructed ashore. During that first terrible winter half of the crew and 44 of the Pilgrims died. Of the 18 wives that left England only four survived the rigor of the New England climate.

19

New York Harbor, 1717.   Scow, Brigantine, Brig, Ketch,

No prophet could have foreseen the future of New York when it was discovered by Verrazano in 1524. Explored by Hudson in 1609, Manhattan Island was colonized by the Dutch in 1625. It was lost to England in 1664, regained by the Dutch in 1673, and finally lost to the English in 1674. At this time the whole coast from Maine to Carolina became a British settlement dependent on rivers and the sea for communication. Intercolonial trade was carried on by water wherever possible, owing to the great difficulty of cutting roads through the vast

Ship, Catboat, and Square-topsail Sloop

forest that covered the country, and the expense of bridging rivers. Situated on its harbor with direct access to the sea, to the rivers leading into New Jersey, the Hudson River, and the East River leading to Long Island Sound, New York was the natural focus of water-borne commerce. Shipbuilding and repairs, ship chandlery, commerce with the interior and overseas made New York in 1717 a bustling center of maritime activity. This scene shows various kinds of vessels that were typical of the day.

21

8 GONDOLAS

2 CUTTERS

3 SCHOONERS

3 GALLEYS

ARNOLD'S FLEET AT THE BATTLE OF VALCOUR BAY

The Stamp Act, trade restrictions, and taxation without representation were some of the many grievances held against England by the American colonists. When open rebellion broke out at Lexington, April 19, 1775, the English realized they had a small war on their hands.

To suppress this revolt they planned to split the colonies in two on a line through Canada to Lake Champlain, then down the Hudson River to New York. Having control of the sea they could separate the rebellious sections and subdue them one by one. Brigadier General Benedict Arnold, who was later to turn traitor, singlehandedly foiled this plan. After the unsuccessful attack on Quebec and Montreal, Arnold and his heroic troops retreated to Ticonderoga on Lake Champlain, where he designed and built a fleet of 16 vessels. He had shipwrights, riggers, sail makers, cannons, ball and powder brought there throughout the winter snows. His fleet carried 88 guns. The British at the upper end of the lake built a fleet of 29 vessels, carrying 89 guns manned by trained crews expert at seamanship and gunnery.

Arnold, knowing the more heavily gunned and better manned British fleet could defeat him in a fight in the open lake, anchored in a cove on the west side of Valcour Island. Protected by shallow water from

22

The Battle of Valcour Bay

behind, his ships were anchored in a crescent with his fire power concentrated at the point where the water was deep enough for the larger British ships to do their maneuvering. Arnold's fleet was so skillfully camouflaged with green boughs that the larger units of the enemy missed his vessels and sailed beyond the island. When the British discovered their error they had difficulty tacking back against the fresh northeast wind. In the meantime, the smaller British gondolas attacked until they were joined later by the whole fleet. The battle raged from 11 A.M. to 5 P.M., at which point the enemy anchored in a line off the island hoping to bottle up Arnold. During the night, under cover of a fog, most of the undamaged American fleet escaped. They were chased down the lake and all but four were sunk or captured. Benedict Arnold lost the battle of Lake Champlain on October 11, 1776, but he gained a year of time for the colonists. They were able to mass at Saratoga in 1777 and defeat General Burgoyne. This was the decisive battle of the war, for it led France, Spain, and Holland to join us. Without their help we would have been quickly overwhelmed. 23

U.S.S. LEXINGTON versus H.M.S. ALERT

Our infant American navy could do little or nothing against the overwhelming naval strength of England during the Revolutionary War. Nevertheless, by 1778 our privateers had captured 1000 British ships worth £2,000,000.

The *Lexington,* formerly a merchant brig named the *Black Duck,* was armed with 16 guns and sent to France to join the privateers *Reprisal* and *Dolphin.* This small squadron operated in the Bay of Biscay and along the entire British coast, taking 15 vessels. Chased by a large English battleship the squadron took refuge in a French port. However, the French were not yet at war with England and the *Lexington* was ordered to leave port.

One day out the *Lexington* fell in with H.M.S. *Alert,* a cutter of 10 guns. Owing to her hasty departure, the *Lexington* was short of ammunition but she fought the *Alert* in an all-day battle in boisterous seas. Captain Johnston of the *Lexington* refused to surrender for an hour after he had run out of ammunition.

The victory at Saratoga had shown the French under Louis XVI that we had power enough to cause England serious trouble. On February 6, 1778, we signed treaties of alliance and commerce with France.

On the 13th of April 12 ships of the line and 5 frigates under Count d'Estaing sailed from Toulon for the American shore under orders to seek out the British and destroy them. Hearing that the English fleet was at Delaware Bay, D'Estaing sailed there but missed them by ten days. He went on to New York but Admiral Howe had lined the Sandy Hook Channel with his ships so that the French fleet would have to run the gantlet of British guns. Despite the fact that the French fleet was bigger and more heavily gunned, D'Estaing refused to do battle and retreated to Newport, where he joined a detachment of Americans camped outside the seaport. The town would have fallen into our hands had not Howe sailed up from New York to protect it. D'Estaing tried to fight the British off Narragansett Bay, but a storm dispersed both fleets. Newport remained in British hands. D'Estaing sailed for Boston, where his fleet spent the winter making repairs.

Primarily the French were only interested in advancing their own cause. The Americans had to fight and win their war themselves. However, if it had not been for outside assistance, no matter how self-centered, we would have been overwhelmed by the British. 25

Count d'Estaing's Fleet at Sea

1. SPANKER BOOM LIFT
2. VANG
3. MAINBRACE
4. CROSSJACK BRACE
5. CROSSJACK YARD LIFT
6. MIZZEN-TOPSAIL SHEET
7. FLAG HALYARD
8. MIZZEN-TOPSAIL BRACE
9. MIZZEN-TOPGALLANT SHEET

10. MIZZEN-TOPSAIL YARD LIFT

11. SPANKER YARD LIFT
12. MAIN-TOPSAIL BRACE
13. MIZZEN-TOPGALLANT BRACE
14. MIZZEN-TOPGALLANT YARD LIFT

15. MAIN-TOPGALLANT BRACE
16. MAIN-TOPGALLANT YARD LIFT
17. FORE-TOPGALLANT BRACE
18. FORE-TOPSAIL BRACE
19. MAIN-TOPGALLANT SHEET
20. MAIN-TOPSAIL YARD LIFT
21. MAIN-TOPSAIL SHEET
22. MAIN-YARD LIFT
23. FOREBRACE
24. FORE-TOPGALLANT YARD LIFT
25. FORE-TOPGALLANT SHEET
26. FORE-TOPSAIL YARD LIFT
27. INNER JIB HALYARD
28. FORE-TOPSAIL SHEET
29. FOREYARD LIFT
30. OUTER JIB HALYARD
31. SPRITSAIL YARD LIFT
32. MIZZEN-YARD BOWLINE

STERN

BOW

1. RUDDER
2. QUARTER GALLERY
3. SPANKER BOOM
4. QUARTERDECK
5. MIZZENMAST
6. MIZZEN SHROUDS
7. MIZZEN-TOPMAST BACKSTAY
8. MIZZEN-TOPGALLANT MAST BACKSTAY
9. CROSSJACK YARD
10. MIZZENTOP
11. SPANKER YARD
12. MIZZEN-TOPSAIL YARD
13. MIZZEN-TOPMAST SHROUDS
14. MIZZEN-TOPMAST
15. MIZZEN-TOPMAST CROSS TREES
16. MIZZEN-TOPGALLANT YARD
17. MIZZEN-TOPGALLANT SHROUDS
18. MIZZEN-TOPGALLANT MAST
19. MIZZEN-TOPGALLANT MAST STAY
20. MIZZEN-TOPMAST STAY
21. MAIN-TOPGALLANT MAST BACKSTAY
22. MAIN-TOPMAST BACKSTAY
23. MIZZEN STAY
24. MAIN SHROUDS
25. MAINMAST
26. MAIN YARD

27. MAIN-TOPMAST STUDDING SAIL BOOM
28. MAINTOP
29. MAIN-TOPSAIL YARD
30. MAIN-TOPGALLANT STUDDING SAIL BOOM
31. MAIN TOPMAST
32. MAIN-TOPMAST SHROUDS
33. MAIN-TOPMAST CROSSTREES
34. MAIN-TOPGALLANT YARD
35. MAIN-TOPGALLANT SHROUDS
36. MAIN-TOPGALLANT MAST
37. MAIN-TOPGALLANT MAST STAY
38. MAIN-TOPMAST STAY
39. MAINSTAYS
40. FORE-TOPGALLANT MAST BACKSTAY
41. FORE-TOPMAST BACK STAY
42. FORESHROUDS
43. FOREMAST
44. FOREYARD

45. FORE-TOPMAST STUDDING SAIL BOOM
46. FORE FUTTOCK SHROUDS
47. FORETOP
48. FORE-TOPGALLANT STUDDING SAIL BOOM
49. FORE-TOPSAIL YARD
50. FORE-TOPMAST SHROUDS
51. FORE-TOPMAST
52. FORE-TOPMAST CROSSTREES
53. FORE-TOPGALLANT YARD
54. FORE-TOPGALLANT SHROUDS
55. FORE-TOPGALLANT MAST
56. FORE-TOPGALLANT MAST STAY
57. OUTER FORE-TOPMAST JIB STAY
58. INNER FORE-TOPMAST JIB STAYS
59. FORESTAY
60. SPRITSAIL TOPSAIL YARD
61. JIB BOOM

62. MARTINGALE STAYS
63. MARTINGALE OR DOLPHIN STRIKER
64. BOBSTAYS
65. SPRITSAIL YARD
66. BOWSPRIT
67. FIGUREHEAD
68. BUMKIN
69. CATHEADS
70. FORECASTLE DECK
71. ANCHOR
72. BITTS
73. SMOKE PIPE OR CHARLIE NOBLE
74. MAIN DECK
75. MAIN HATCH
76. MAIN COMPANIONWAY
77. CAPSTAN
78. WHEEL AND BINNACLE
79. BOARDING LADDER AND BARREL
80. WALE
81. CHANNELS
82. GUN PORTS
83. PORT LIDS
84. BOTTOM

The Frigate RALEIGH, 1776

U.S.S. RALEIGH *versus* H.M.S. UNICORN *and* H.M.S. EXPERIMENT

The excellent design of the *Raleigh* was as typical of the frigates built during the Revolution as was her fate. The American colonists were fine seamen, fishermen, and commercial seafarers. But they lacked at this time the training and absolute discipline necessary to command and engage another man-of-war in battle.

The *Raleigh* and a converted merchantman, the *Alfred,* sailed for France in September, 1776, to get needed military supplies for the American army. On the way across they met a convoy and captured two ships. Then they tried to take the three ships guarding the convoy but were beaten off. On their return from France they fell in with two smaller British warships. The *Alfred* was captured and the *Raleigh's* commander, not willing to risk his valuable cargo in battle, fled.

In 1778, under Captain John Barry, the *Raleigh* while escorting two merchant ships was chased by the 28-gun *Unicorn* and the 50-gun *Experiment.* The *Raleigh* and the *Unicorn* battled until the *Experiment* caught up to them. Overpowered, Barry ran his ship ashore on Wooden Ball Island off the Penobscot River. 27

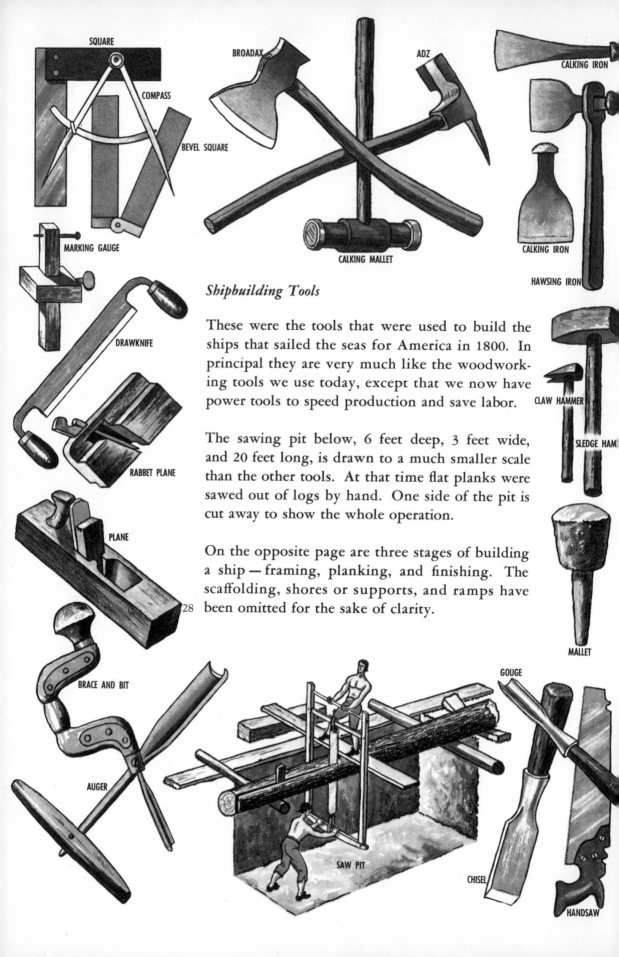

Shipbuilding Tools

These were the tools that were used to build the ships that sailed the seas for America in 1800. In principal they are very much like the woodworking tools we use today, except that we now have power tools to speed production and save labor.

The sawing pit below, 6 feet deep, 3 feet wide, and 20 feet long, is drawn to a much smaller scale than the other tools. At that time flat planks were sawed out of logs by hand. One side of the pit is cut away to show the whole operation.

On the opposite page are three stages of building a ship — framing, planking, and finishing. The scaffolding, shores or supports, and ramps have been omitted for the sake of clarity.

28

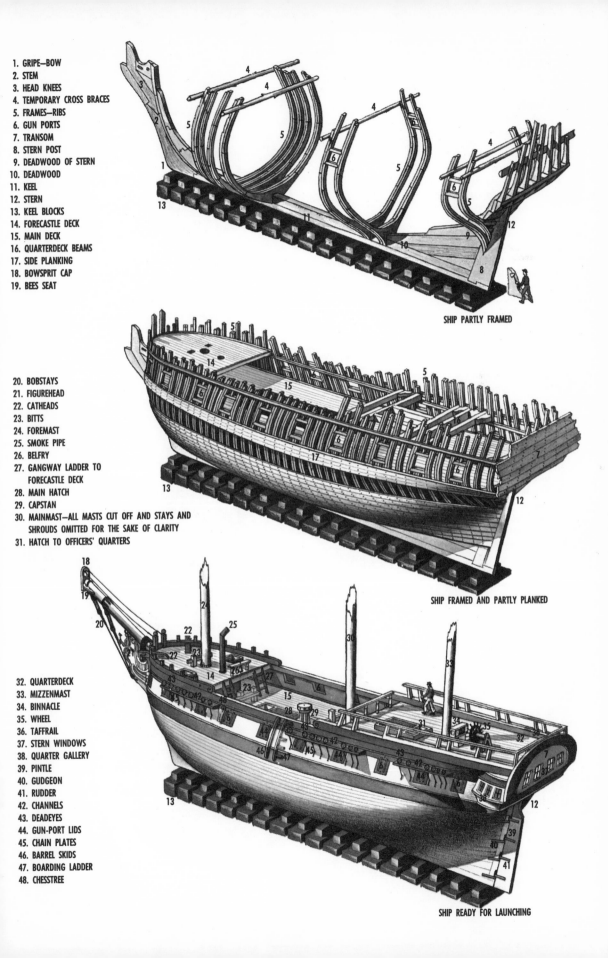

1. GRIPE—BOW
2. STEM
3. HEAD KNEES
4. TEMPORARY CROSS BRACES
5. FRAMES—RIBS
6. GUN PORTS
7. TRANSOM
8. STERN POST
9. DEADWOOD OF STERN
10. DEADWOOD
11. KEEL
12. STERN
13. KEEL BLOCKS
14. FORECASTLE DECK
15. MAIN DECK
16. QUARTERDECK BEAMS
17. SIDE PLANKING
18. BOWSPRIT CAP
19. BEES SEAT

20. BOBSTAYS
21. FIGUREHEAD
22. CATHEADS
23. BITTS
24. FOREMAST
25. SMOKE PIPE
26. BELFRY
27. GANGWAY LADDER TO
    FORECASTLE DECK
28. MAIN HATCH
29. CAPSTAN
30. MAINMAST—ALL MASTS CUT OFF AND STAYS AND
    SHROUDS OMITTED FOR THE SAKE OF CLARITY
31. HATCH TO OFFICERS' QUARTERS

32. QUARTERDECK
33. MIZZENMAST
34. BINNACLE
35. WHEEL
36. TAFFRAIL
37. STERN WINDOWS
38. QUARTER GALLERY
39. PINTLE
40. GUDGEON
41. RUDDER
42. CHANNELS
43. DEADEYES
44. GUN-PORT LIDS
45. CHAIN PLATES
46. BARREL SKIDS
47. BOARDING LADDER
48. CHESSTREE

SHIP PARTLY FRAMED

SHIP FRAMED AND PARTLY PLANKED

SHIP READY FOR LAUNCHING

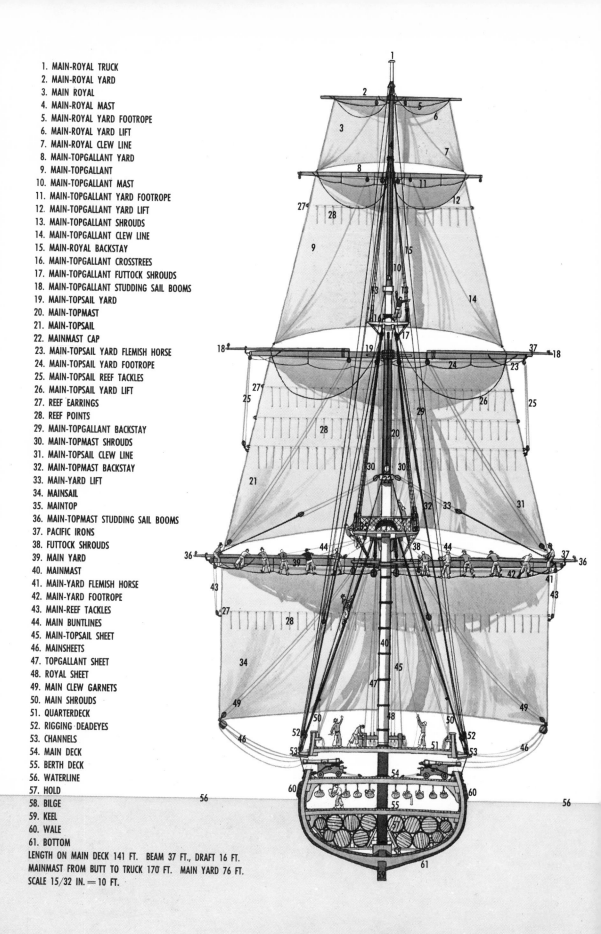

1. MAIN-ROYAL TRUCK
2. MAIN-ROYAL YARD
3. MAIN ROYAL
4. MAIN-ROYAL MAST
5. MAIN-ROYAL YARD FOOTROPE
6. MAIN-ROYAL YARD LIFT
7. MAIN-ROYAL CLEW LINE
8. MAIN-TOPGALLANT YARD
9. MAIN-TOPGALLANT
10. MAIN-TOPGALLANT MAST
11. MAIN-TOPGALLANT YARD FOOTROPE
12. MAIN-TOPGALLANT YARD LIFT
13. MAIN-TOPGALLANT SHROUDS
14. MAIN-TOPGALLANT CLEW LINE
15. MAIN-ROYAL BACKSTAY
16. MAIN-TOPGALLANT CROSSTREES
17. MAIN-TOPGALLANT FUTTOCK SHROUDS
18. MAIN-TOPGALLANT STUDDING SAIL BOOMS
19. MAIN-TOPSAIL YARD
20. MAIN-TOPMAST
21. MAIN-TOPSAIL
22. MAINMAST CAP
23. MAIN-TOPSAIL YARD FLEMISH HORSE
24. MAIN-TOPSAIL YARD FOOTROPE
25. MAIN-TOPSAIL REEF TACKLES
26. MAIN-TOPSAIL YARD LIFT
27. REEF EARRINGS
28. REEF POINTS
29. MAIN-TOPGALLANT BACKSTAY
30. MAIN-TOPMAST SHROUDS
31. MAIN-TOPSAIL CLEW LINE
32. MAIN-TOPMAST BACKSTAY
33. MAIN-YARD LIFT
34. MAINSAIL
35. MAINTOP
36. MAIN-TOPMAST STUDDING SAIL BOOMS
37. PACIFIC IRONS
38. FUTTOCK SHROUDS
39. MAIN YARD
40. MAINMAST
41. MAIN-YARD FLEMISH HORSE
42. MAIN-YARD FOOTROPE
43. MAIN-REEF TACKLES
44. MAIN BUNTLINES
45. MAIN-TOPSAIL SHEET
46. MAINSHEETS
47. TOPGALLANT SHEET
48. ROYAL SHEET
49. MAIN CLEW GARNETS
50. MAIN SHROUDS
51. QUARTERDECK
52. RIGGING DEADEYES
53. CHANNELS
54. MAIN DECK
55. BERTH DECK
56. WATERLINE
57. HOLD
58. BILGE
59. KEEL
60. WALE
61. BOTTOM

LENGTH ON MAIN DECK 141 FT. BEAM 37 FT., DRAFT 16 FT.
MAINMAST FROM BUTT TO TRUCK 170 FT. MAIN YARD 76 FT.
SCALE 15/32 IN. = 10 FT.

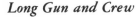

Long Gun and Crew

On the opposite page is a ship of 1800, cut away just aft of the mainmast, to show the rigging and hull.

Above is a long gun and the crew required to handle it. When guns on both sides of the ship were being fired, the first loaders stayed on one side of the ship and the seconds went to the cannon on the opposite side.

Below (the carronade cut away), the essential parts of both cannon and carronade are shown. The carronade was the lighter gun of the two, having a shorter barrel with the same bore as a cannon. Being lighter, it was used on the upper decks so that the ship would not be top heavy. Its range was shorter than that of a cannon firing the same-weight cannon ball.

31

Cutaway of a 12-pound Carronade

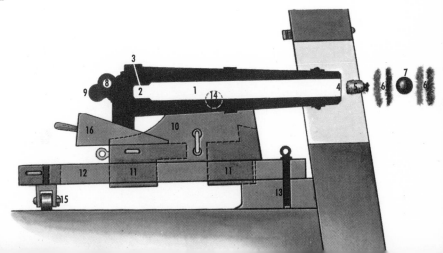

The U.S.S. CONSTITUTION Bombarding Tripoli,

On October 21, 1797, the most famous vessel in the American navy was launched from the Hartt yard in Boston, where she was christened *Constitution.* She and her two sister ships, the *President* and the *United States,* were designed by Joshua Humphreys, who evolved a type of vessel unique among frigates and 15 years ahead of their time. Their speed, maneuverability, and seaworthiness made them superior to any of the same class in European navies.

At this time the great powers were at war. Revolutionary France and England were engaged in a life-and-death struggle. The French revolutionists, having no respect for international law, were seizing American ships engaged in trade with England. By 1798 we were in an undeclared war with the French. This war started our young navy on its ironbound system of discipline necessary for training men and officers for successful naval combat.

August 3, 1804

The *Constitution's* first occupation was to cruise to the West Indies with the United States fleet. No sooner was the quasi-war with France settled then we got into a war with the Barbary pirates, who from their strongholds on the southern shore of the Mediterranean were seizing American ships and holding the crews in slavery for ransom. The time spent thrashing the Barbary pirates afforded further training for our navy. Commodore Edward Preble's fleet has been called the nursery of the navy, for a majority of the officers who were to distinguish themselves in the war of 1812 served under Preble in the Mediterranean war with the Barbary pirates.

The *Constitution* was the flagship of the Mediterranean squadron from 1803 to 1807. During this time she bombarded the Tripolitan forts, destroyed the fleet of the Bey of Tunis, and brought about his signing a treaty to abolish ransom and tribute.

33

Derby's Wharf, Salem, 1808

The seaport of Salem, Massachusetts, had its heyday following the Revolutionary War. Founded in 1626, Salem was by 1643 a thriving seaport exporting salted fish and lumber to the West Indies and bringing back sugar and molasses. During the Revolution, Salem was the only important port that was not captured by the British. As a result Salem sent out large numbers of privateers which made great fortunes for their owners and crews. After the war the same ships scoured the world for new markets ushering in the first great era of American foreign trade. Nathaniel Bowditch, navigator and mathematical genius, was born here in 1773, and here before he was thirty he wrote *The New American Practical Navigator,* the book that comes next to the Bible in every navigator's heart. In 1812, Salem again sent out more privateers, making new fortunes. After the war, as ships got bigger and drew more water, Salem began its decline, for its harbor was too small and shallow for the big new ships.

When the United States bought the Louisiana territory from France in 1803, a vast new trade artery was introduced. All the rivers of the central part of the country were opened to trade and commerce.

Rafts of logs drifted downstream, sometimes all the way to New Orleans; flatboats and crude skows made of rough lumber rode the current down the rivers loaded with the produce of the new frontier. The crews lived aboard — cooked in sandboxes, hunted game ashore, caught fish and turtles — and had only to man the long sweeps that kept them in the main current. At their destinations, the rafts and flatboats were broken up for use as building lumber and the cargoes sold. Often the crew walked home or worked on a keelboat for the upstream passage.

The keelboats were well-formed vessels that could be rowed, or towed from shore by men pulling on the tow rope, or they could be poled by the crew walking along the side decks pushing on poles, or even sailed in favorable winds. It took three months of back-breaking labor to bring twenty tons of cargo from New Orleans to St. Louis. The crew lived in part of the shelter, where they slept in rough board bunks and cooked in a fireplace. The cargo took up the rest of the space in the shelter. Added to the incessant toil was the ever present danger of an Indian raid — a crew scalped, the cargo stolen, and the boat burned.

35

Keelboat, Flatboat, and Raft

John Fitch, 1787

James Rumsey, 1787

John Stevens, 1802

Oliver Evans, 1803

In 1707 the first steamboat in the world was invented and built by Denis Papin in Kassel (now West Germany). It operated with moderate success on the Weser River. Unfortunately, it was destroyed soon after being built, by river boatmen who thought a steamboat would put them out of work.

America's first steamboat was built and operated by John Fitch at Philadelphia, in October, 1787. The event was considered so important that Congress adjourned to witness it. The vessel was a crude affair propelled by crank-driven paddles.

Three months later, James Rumsey's jet-driven steamer operated on the Potomac. It had a steam-driven pump that sucked water in at the bow and ejected it forcibly at the stern.

In 1802, John Stevens invented the first propeller-driven steamboat. His vessel was far ahead of its time, having a high-pressure boiler and a reliable engine. It was not until after 1836 that the efficient propeller superseded the paddle wheel and was accepted by shipowners and designers.

In 1803, Oliver Evans, an early American mechanical genius, designed and built the first steam amphibian. The skow-type hull supported a high-pressure boiler and engine. Four large iron wheels propelled the device on land and a paddle wheel at the stern moved it in the water. It was used as a dredge to deepen the harbor at Philadelphia.

Robert Fulton's famous *Clermont,* variously known as the *Katherine of Clermont* and/or the *North River Steamboat of Clermont,* was the first steam vessel to be successful commercially.

Robert Fulton was a man of many talents; artist, inventor, and engineer, he built a manually operated submarine for Napoleon and a steamboat in 1803 that operated with fair success on the Seine in Paris. Fulton's *Clermont* was built on New York's East River at the Charles Browne shipyard near Corlaer's Hook. It was an ordinary flat-bottomed river boat, with parallel sides and no deck, a transom stern, and a pointed bow with a small cabin on it. The English Boulton and Watt single cylinder steam engine with its cranks and gears was in the open hull, just as was the large low pressure boiler on its reinforced brick base.

On August 17, 1807, the steamboat left the pier on the Hudson River near Greenwich Village with a group of distinguished guests aboard, very few of whom thought the boat would make the trip. After a hesitant start, the steamboat sailed triumphantly to Clermont and then to Albany.

The day of rapid steam transportation by water had arrived.   37

The CLERMONT on the Hudson River, 1807

The CONSTITUTION and the GUERRIÈRE

It is difficult to realize today that the United States of America was once a small nation too weak to maintain her neutrality with the warring French and British. We were unable to prevent the British from impressing our seamen into their tremendous navy. In 1812, with 17 ships ready for sea, we challenged this powerful country that had about 650 well-armed, expertly manned and officered ships. Almost at once Britain declared a blockade on our coast, which was only partially successful because most of their ships were fighting Napoleon's fleets. By 1813 the Napoleonic naval power was on the decline so the British fleet was able to blockade the whole coast effectively. After two years of this blockade American trade and water-borne commerce was at a standstill.

Some ships however managed to slip out through the blockade. Among these the frigate *Constitution*, 55 guns, commanded by Captain Isaac Hull met the *Guerrière*, 49 guns, on August 19, 1812, in the first major naval battle of the war. The *Constitution*, by virtue of her better gunnery, disabled the *Guerrière* by shooting her mizzenmast out. She was raked again and again. When all her masts had been shot away she surrendered. This victory helped the morale of the country, particularly in New England, where the *Constitution* had been built.

38

Standing on the deck of the disabled brig *Lawrence,* Master Commandant Oliver Hazard Perry wrote this famous dispatch on the back of an old envelope: "We have met the enemy — and they are ours — 2 ships, 2 brigs, 1 schooner and 1 sloop." In the winter of 1813, Oliver Hazard Perry had been sent to Lake Erie to organize and command the American units there. A fleet was built at Erie from all kinds of makeshift materials. It was manned by a nucleus of navy men, some soldiers, and a motley crew of trappers, frontiersmen, and anyone who could be snatched aboard. While anchored at Put-in-Bay in the Bass Islands, Perry's fleet sighted the British ships sailing down the lake in light winds. The American fleet of nine vessels came out as fast as the feeble wind permitted. The first to meet the six British ships was Perry's flagship, the brig *Lawrence,* 20 guns. The faint breeze prevented the American ships at the end of the line from coming to help those at the forward end. When the *Lawrence* was cut to pieces, Perry transferred his flag to the brig *Niagara,* sister ship of the *Lawrence.* The rest of the fleet came up and forced the British, hopelessly outmatched, to surrender after a gallant defense. 39

The H.M.S. DETROIT versus the U.S.S. LAWRENCE, Battle of Lake Erie

The U.S.S. ESSEX Careened at Nukahiva

The frigate *Essex,* financed by popular subscription and built by Enos Briggs at Salem in 1799, made the most extraordinary cruise of the war. Contrary to the usual procedure of arming a frigate with long guns on the main deck and carronades on the quarterdeck, the *Essex* was armed with forty 32-pound carronades on both decks and six long 12-pounders at bow and stern. This was not pleasing to her Captain, David Porter, but more long guns were unavailable, for in the young country at that time there were very few iron foundries equipped to handle the complicated task of casting cannon.

Sailing from Delaware Bay on October 27, 1812, the *Essex* expected to cruise in squadron with the *Constitution* and the *Hornet* in the South Atlantic. On the way to the rendezvous she captured the British packet *Nocton,* carrying £11,000, and sent her to America with a prize crew.

The *Essex* missed the rendezvous just north of Rio de Janeiro and sailed south rounding Cape Horn to Valparaiso, Chile, where water and stores were taken aboard. On leaving Valparaiso, the *Essex* captured a Peruvian corsair with 24 imprisoned American whalemen aboard. Proceeding to the Galápagos whaling grounds the *Essex* captured 12 British whalers in six months, disrupting the English whaling trade in that area.

Since the ship had been at sea for a year the bottom was in need of scraping. In company with some of her prizes she went to Nukahiva in the Marquesas, where she was careened, cleaned (thousands of rats were driven out of her hold) and recalked.

The refurbished ship sailed for Valparaiso, arriving January 12, 1814. Here the British ships *Phoebe,* 36 guns, and the *Cherub,* 18 guns, were waiting for the *Essex,* having been sent out especially to take her. Since Valparaiso was a neutral port, hostilities did not begin until the *Essex* was blown offshore in a squall after her anchor cable parted. The *Phoebe* with her long 18-pound guns was able to keep out of the range of the American's carronades and proceeded to pound the *Essex* to pieces. Porter, his guns useless, his rigging destroyed, his crew of 250 reduced to 76 unwounded, surrendered on March 28, after a battle that lasted two and one-half hours. 41

The ESSEX Captured off Valparaiso, 1814

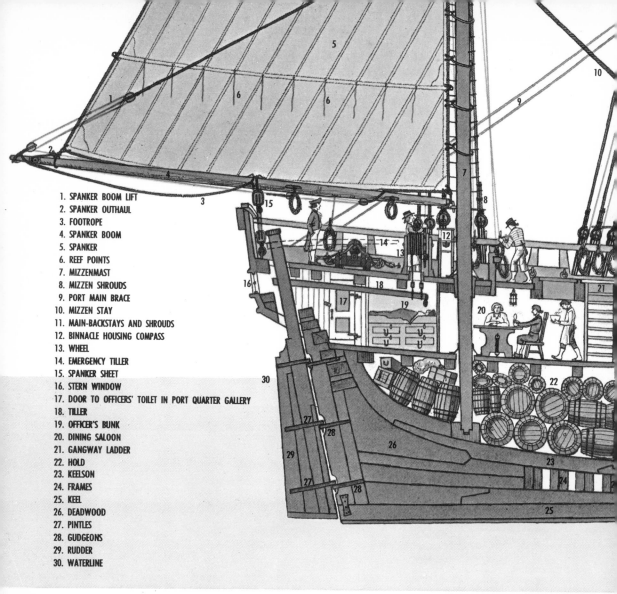

1. SPANKER BOOM LIFT
2. SPANKER OUTHAUL
3. FOOTROPE
4. SPANKER BOOM
5. SPANKER
6. REEF POINTS
7. MIZZENMAST
8. MIZZEN SHROUDS
9. PORT MAIN BRACE
10. MIZZEN STAY
11. MAIN-BACKSTAYS AND SHROUDS
12. BINNACLE HOUSING COMPASS
13. WHEEL
14. EMERGENCY TILLER
15. SPANKER SHEET
16. STERN WINDOW
17. DOOR TO OFFICERS' TOILET IN PORT QUARTER GALLERY
18. TILLER
19. OFFICER'S BUNK
20. DINING SALOON
21. GANGWAY LADDER
22. HOLD
23. KEELSON
24. FRAMES
25. KEEL
26. DEADWOOD
27. PINTLES
28. GUDGEONS
29. RUDDER
30. WATERLINE

Cutaway of a Ship's Stern

Following the War of 1812, there was a great resurgence of commercial activity in shipping. Many Americans went to sea, for there rested the biggest chances for success in these times. The section of a ship's stern drawn above shows what has become popularly known today as "officer country": the ultimate goal of every aspiring young seaman. The starboard side of the quarterdeck was reserved for the Captain. Here he got his exercise by pacing forward and aft while the mates kept to the port side. Foremast hands were only tolerated here to steer, clean, and work the ship. The ship section shown was of a 300-ton merchant vessel about 90 feet long.

Considered by modern standards, these ships were floating torture chambers. The perils of the sea were ever present. Men fell out of the rigging in storms too violent to permit a boat to be lowered to pick them up, or men were washed overboard by big seas.

On a warship of 1812, 450 men were crowded into a ship 175 feet long. The crew lived like kenneled dogs, having a space 22 inches wide by 8 feet long in which to hang a hammock. On a long voyage the men often got scurvy and in bad weather there was no ventilation or way to dry clothes, so respiratory infections were commonplace.

Toilet facilities for the crew at the head of the ship consisted of four seats of ease on which the men sat. At sea the plunging of the ship kept this area clean but this was not always the case in port.

After the first few days at sea all provisions were dried or salted. One ship's cook took care of 450 men. A mess boy was assigned to a mess of 10 men. He drew provisions from the purser, marked his hunk of salt pork or beef to be boiled in the coppers of the galley, served the meal on the square black mess cloth, and cleaned the mess kits and utensils in salt water without soap.

The weekly ration per man on United States ships in 1812 was 3½ pounds of salt beef, 3 pounds of salt pork, 6 pounds of dried bread (including maggots), 1 quart of rice, 1 pound of flour, ½ pound of fat, 1 pint of dried peas, 6 ounces of cheese (including the worms usually found in it), ½ pint of vinegar, and ½ pint of molasses. Half a pint of whiskey or rum served per day helped kill the bad taste of water that had been in a cask too long.   43

Stern of a Ship   *Bow of a Ship*

1. STERN WINDOWS
2. TRANSOM
3. TAFFRAIL
4. QUARTER GALLERY
5. CHANNEL
6. CHAIN PLATES
7. WHEEL AND BINNACLE
8. MIZZENMAST
9. MIZZEN SHROUDS
10. FOREMAST
11. FORESHROUDS
12. FORESTAY
13. CATHEADS
14. BOWSPRIT
15. BOBSTAYS
16. GAMMONING
17. HAWSEHOLES
18. HEADRAILS
19. SEATS OF EASE
20. FORECASTLE DECK
21. BITTS

STERN VIEW   BOW VIEW

A Whaler in the South Pacific

Until Edwin L. Drake struck oil in Pennsylvania in 1869, houses were lighted by candles and whale-oil lamps. To get this whale oil and candle wax, whaling ships combed the seas for whales. Medium-sized, bluff-bowed, and sturdy, these ships carried a crew of from 25 to 35 men, four or five whaleboats on davits, and two spares on a rack midships.

On sighting a whale from the lookout the man yelled, "Thar she blo-ows." Immediately the boats were lowered and the chase was on. After the whale was harpooned and lanced it was taken alongside the ship, where the blubber was stripped off in a spiral strip, cut up, and boiled in the try-pots on deck to extract the oil. After being cooled the oil was barreled and stowed in the hold.

The profits of a whaling voyage were divided by a system of lays or shares. The owners, a few investors, the captain, and crew received a lay varying anywhere from 1/17th, for the Master, to 1/175th for the lowest foremast hand. Often a whaling voyage lasted four years. A lucky ship might come back with a cargo worth $250,000. But on an unlucky ship a seaman who had spent four years at hard and dangerous work could get as little as $10.

The S.S. FRONTENAC, 1816

While sailing vessels were predominant on the seas, steamships were appearing more and more on the horizon. For example, the first steamer on the Great Lakes was the *Frontenac,* built near Kingston, Canada, in 1816. She was employed on Lake Ontario, carrying freight and passengers between Niagara and Ogdensburg. The second was the *Ontario,* built at Sackets Harbor, New York, in 1817.

These early Great Lake steamers were built much like the seagoing vessels of the time, for the lakes can be as rough and as dangerous as any body of water anywhere. It was not until the bulk carrier *R. J. Hackett* was built in 1869, that lake steamers became the specialized types they are today.

45

The Chicago Line Steamship CONSTELLATION, 1838

The Long Island Sound Steamer CLEOPATRA, 1840

The eighteen-forties were the halcyon days of steamboating. The railroads merely served as feeder lines for the steamers, bringing them passengers and freight from inland points.

The *Cleopatra* was built for Commodore Cornelius Vanderbilt's steamboat lines, which thrived long before he turned to railroading. These vessels were able to steam at 15 knots; they were very comfortable and served excellent and copious meals. As a safety measure the boilers were placed outboard on the sponsons or outboard guardrails so that if they blew up there would be less danger to the passengers. The walking-beam engine shown below was the type generally used to propel these ships. The engines were so durable and well made that they often held up for fifty years, outlasting the hulls of two or three ships.

46

A Walking Beam Engine, 1845

1. WALKING BEAM
2. BEAM BEARINGS
3. "A" FRAME
4. MAIN ROD
5. PADDLE WHEEL
6. MAIN CRANK
7. ECCENTRICS
8. VALVE CAMS
9. MAIN CYLINDER
10. PISTON ROD
11. ENGINE ROOM OPERATING PLATFORM
12. ENGINE ROOM TELEGRAPH
13. VACUUM PUMP
14. TIE RODS
15. VALVES
16. CROSSHEAD
17. LINKAGE RODS
18. STEAM PIPE

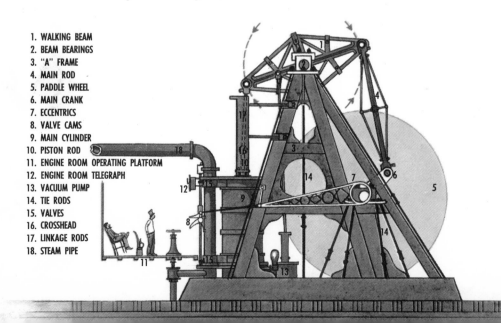

The Mississippi River Steamer BROOKLYN, 1848

The most comfortable and the quickest way to get from Pittsburgh, Pennsylvania, to St. Paul, Minnesota, in 1848, was by river steamer. The journey could be made by stagecoach but it would have taken twice as long and have been decidedly uncomfortable.

In order to navigate the shallow-river waters the steamers were flat-bottomed, of very light draught, many drawing less than 36 inches. This enabled them to lie close to the bank when taking on or discharging passengers and cargo over their long gangplanks, for docks were impractical on the rivers because of the seasonal changes in water level.

On the highest, or hurricane, deck, the raised pilothouse was just aft of the stacks. Immediately behind the pilothouse was the Texas (officers') quarters. The next deck down, the boiler deck — actually the deck above the boilers — had the main saloon or dining cabin, surrounded by 30 passenger cabins each accommodating two people. Aft at the stern was the ladies' cabin. On the main deck, along with the cargo, 200 steerage passengers could be bedded down. The boilers were on the main deck under the stacks. The engine room was between the paddle wheels and the galley at the stern. No cargo was carried in the hull below the main deck.

47

Hudson River Sloop, Paddle-wheel Tug, Packet Ship,

New York Harbor in 1850, was the busiest and most prosperous port in America. The Hudson River sloops, those capacious, shallow-draught center-boarders, carried cargo up and down the Hudson, in the bays, and on Long Island Sound. Paddle-wheel tugs bustled about, docking ships and towing barges. Packet ships, fast and weatherly vessels, made regular voyages to Europe but they were being displaced by the more reliable steam ocean liners that could make the passage from New York to Liverpool in twelve days. Swift and graceful pilot

48

Side-wheel Ocean Liner, and Pilot Schooner, 1850

schooners sailed out past Sandy Hook, putting pilots on incoming ships and taking them off outgoing vessels. The yacht *America,* built on the lines of these pilot schooners, beat the whole British fleet at Cowes, England, in 1851, to win the America's Cup in the first of the famed cup races.

Though it is not shown in this scene, South Street on the East River was so densely packed with docked ships loading and unloading that it looked like a forest of masts.

49

The Ship QUEEN OF CLIPPERS, 1854

    Our American clipper ships were the most beautiful ships that ever sailed the seas. Of simple functional hull forms, with a minimum of decoration, they were mounted by a tall perfectly proportioned rig. They were built chiefly for speed, and pushed by hard-driving captains and mates to the limit of their capabilities. Competition between shipping firms was great; the company having the fastest ship got the best cargoes and the highest rates. The Gold Rush to California gave the clippers great publicity; captains who made record passages were acclaimed as heroes when they reached port. Clippers have sometimes been disparaged as the most over-advertised ships in maritime history, and as scanty cargo carriers for their length.

American ships acquired a bad reputation during the clipper-ship era. The captains were ruthless and reckless sail carriers. The mates were selected for their abilities to overwork and bully the crew as well as for their seamanship. The pay was low, the food poor, and the hardships of a voyage so unbelievable that very few American seamen sailed on these ships. The owners tried to justify the brutal conduct of the officers by saying that fast passages were the most important consideration and that the men before the mast were dock rats who responded only to the law of brute force.

Few of the clippers were seaworthy after ten years of hard driving. More efficient and reliable steamers further contributed to their oblivion. 51

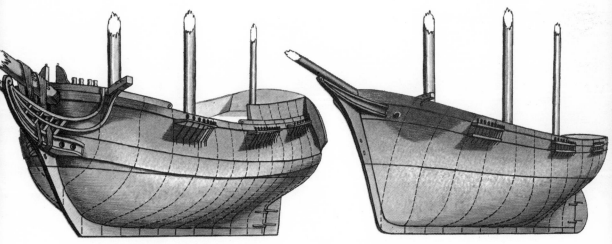

Full-bodied Ship

Bluff-bowed, much carved woodwork at bow, sides tumbled home (curved inward above waterline), very fine lines aft, so water could come easily to rudder, high sides and poop, wide channels to give spread for shrouds.

Clipper Ship

Long sharp bow, no ornament at bow, slightly hollow below waterline, flatter floors and sharp turn to bilge, fine lines aft, note lower silhouette and racy look.

To escape the British and American patrol ships trying to suppress the slave trade, the slaver had to be faster than the ship chasing her. Further, in order that the slaves reach this country in healthy condition, the voyage had to be made as quickly as possible.

After being captured in Africa, the slaves were sold to the captain or owner of a slave ship. Chained to the deck of the hold in long rows in a sitting position, the slaves could lie down but could not stand up. Once a day a small group at a time were unchained and sent up on deck for exercise and food. Here they were kept under constant guard, for fear that they would commit suicide by jumping over the side or rebel and kill the officers and crew. On an average voyage, out of a cargo of 200 slaves, 50 would die of disease or other causes.

Not until the outbreak of the Civil War was this despicable form of trade eradicated.

The Hermaphrodite Brig Slaver L'ANTONIO

The U.S.S. MISSISSIPPI and the Ship of the Line U.S.S. NORTH CAROLINA

On April 12, 1861, the first gun of the Civil War was fired by the Confederate battery on James Island at Fort Sumter in Charleston Harbor. At this time the Union navy had 42 vessels commissioned and ready for active service. Half of these were wooden steam-driven ships with auxiliary sail, and the rest were wooden sailing ships. Eighteen of the best Northern ships were on foreign station. The first task of the Union navy was to blockade all Southern ports from Texas to Norfolk, Virginia. By buying and arming all sorts of ships new or old, and by building a fleet of 23 gunboats in 90 days, the Union was able to hold the South in the tightest blockade in history.

The Southern Confederate States, dependent on outside sources for most of their manufactured goods, were slowly strangled by the Union blockade.

Nevertheless, the Union forces in charge of the Norfolk Navy Yard suspected that the Southern forces would attempt to attack the Yard, which because of indecision and misunderstanding was not properly defended. Rather than have their material and ships fall into Southern hands, the Union forces burned quantities of their naval supplies, 2 sloops of war, 3 frigates, 4 old battleships of the line, and the powerful steam frigate *Merrimac.* Only the sloop of war *Cumberland* escaped. Although the *Merrimac* had burned to the water's edge and sunk, she was salvaged by the South and converted into the powerful ironclad, *Virginia,* which nearly turned the tide of naval warfare in the favor of the Confederate States. 53

The C.S.S. VIRGINIA (formerly MERRIMAC) versus the U.S. MONITOR

An entirely new era in naval architecture and sea warfare was ushered in on March 9, 1862, when the Confederate ironclad *Virginia*, formerly the *Merrimac*, fought the Northern ironclad turret ship *Monitor* to a draw.

The *Virginia*'s sloping sides were built of pine 20 inches thick sheathed with four inches of oak planking. This was covered with two layers of iron bars each two inches thick. The inside layer was placed horizontally and the outside layer vertically. Within this structure she carried three nine-inch smooth-bore Dahlgren guns and one Brooke rifled gun on each side, plus a rifled seven-inch gun at bow and stern. Her engine had been damaged by the fire so she could only steam at five knots. The great weight of her armor caused her to draw 22 feet and to steer badly.

LENGTH OVER-ALL 173 FT.

1. STERN	5. AIR INTAKE PORT & STARBOARD	9. TWO RETURN-TUBE "BOX" BOILERS	13. REVOLVING TURRET
2. BALANCED RUDDER	6. DOUBLE TRUNK ENGINE	10. ENGINE & GEARING TO REVOLVE TURRET	14. CREW'S QUARTERS
3. PROPELLER WELL	7. ENGINE & BOILER ROOM	11. GALLEY	15. OFFICERS' QUARTERS
4. 4-BLADED PROPELLER	8. SMOKE VENT PORT & STARBOARD	12. SWINGING GUN-PORT SHUTTERS	16. CAPTAIN'S QUARTERS

Longitudinal Cross Section of the MONITOR

The *Monitor* was Swedish-born John Ericsson's creation from stem to stern. Every piece of mechanical equipment on the ship was invented or designed by him. Her low flat hull had only one and one-half feet of free board. The steam-driven revolving turret was in the center of the vessel, turning on a large spindle so that the guns could be fired in any direction. She had two muzzle-loading Dahlgren guns mounted on recoil-absorbing tracks. Heavy iron shutters covered the gun ports during reloading. A small elevator lifted powder and shot from the lower part of the ship to the turret. The anchor could be raised and lowered from inside the ship to keep the crew safe under fire. Her engine drove her at eight knots and the large balanced rudder steered the ship so that she could maneuver quickly. Air for the boilers and crew was drawn in through two deck vents by steam-driven fans. Smoke from the boilers was ejected through two grated openings in the deck.

The *Monitor*'s fatal weakness was that she was not seaworthy. Her low freeboard permitted water to enter the deck openings for ventilation and smoke exhaust, thus putting out her fires and nearly sinking her on her voyage from New York, where she was built, to the Chesapeake. After the battle, smoke stacks and higher air-intake vents were installed, plus an arrangement that allowed her to be steered from the top of her turret. But in a very bad storm off Cape Hatteras she sank, taking with her four men and one officer. The *Virginia*'s fate was equally dismal, for she was blown up by her own people when the Union army threatened her on the James River.

55

Cross Section of the MONITOR at the Turret

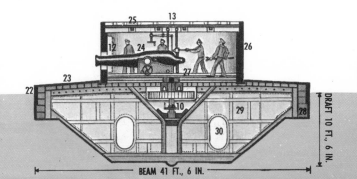

17. PILOTHOUSE	24. TWO 11-INCH DAHLGREN GUNS
18. ANCHOR WINDLASS	25. IRON GRATING
19. ANCHOR IN WELL	26. 8-INCH TURRET ARMOR
20. BOW	27. RECOIL ABSORBING TRACKS
21. KEEL	28. WOOD BACKING TO ARMOR
22. WATERLINE ARMOR	29. TRANSVERSE BULKHEAD
23. 1-INCH DECK ARMOR	30. ACCESS PORTS

BEAM 41 FT., 6 IN.

DRAFT 10 FT., 6 IN.

Dahlgren Pivot Gun, 1863

Most of the naval engagements of the Civil War were fought with muzzle-loading smooth-bore guns like the one above. The shot of a 15-inch gun had an effective range of three miles. Except for size these guns were very much like the guns used since 1600.

The ironclad *Tennessee* was the pride of the Confederate navy. Built at Selma, near Montgomery, on the Alabama River, she was launched early in 1864. At the battle of Mobile Bay she took on the whole Northern squadron, causing tremendous damage, but was finally captured in the face of overpowering odds.

56

The C.S.S. Ram TENNESSEE, 1864

The C.S.S. ALABAMA versus the U.S.S. KEARSARGE

Well-armed fast auxiliary steamers sailed the seven seas during the Civil War, destroying Union shipping and causing marine insurance rates to skyrocket.

The British-built *Alabama* was the most successful of all the Confederate commerce raiders. Under the command of Captain Raphael Semmes she captured or destroyed 70 vessels, whose crews were treated with care and consideration.

After her brilliant cruise the *Alabama* put into Cherbourg, France, for supplies. She was challenged to a battle by Captain Ralph Winslow of the U.S.S. *Kearsarge,* one of the many Union vessels sent out to "get" the *Alabama.*

On June 19, 1864, the battle took place seven miles off Cherbourg. Thousands of people watched from the hills on shore as the two ships steamed in circles, firing continuously. After seven circles the *Kearsarge* by virtue of greater fire power sank the *Alabama.* Semmes and his crew were picked up by a British yacht, thus avoiding capture by the Northern forces.

57

The Ohio River Towboat IRON AGE, 1877

The Mississippi River steamer on page 47 and the vessels on these two pages are unique American inventions. The shallow waters of the western river systems required flat shoal hulls and great power to buck the strong downstream currents. The first typical river steamer was the *Washington*, built by Henry Shreve in 1816. She was a flat-bottomed shallow-draft boat with her engine on deck turning side-wheel paddles. Over the years the side-wheelers evolved into ornate floating palaces that were eventually supplanted by the faster railroad cars. However, the workaday stern-wheelers, plain and utilitarian like the *Iron Age*, could tow great floats of loaded barges, carrying vast tonnages, much more cheaply than the railroads could per tonnage mile.

On the rivers "towing" is really "pushing." With the tow forward it is easier to steer and water resistance is lowered by having the barges ahead out of the wake of the paddle wheel.

This beautiful little deep-draft side-wheel steam ferry, the *San Rafael*, brings back visions of the great days of steamboating on America's inland waters.

From the Gold Rush days of 1849 to 1936 when the ferries were supplanted by bridges, San Francisco Bay and its tributaries were crisscrossed by passenger steamers. The *San Rafael* was built in sections by the North River Iron Works of New York and shipped around the Horn in a sailing ship to San Francisco. There she was assembled to carry passengers between the ferry terminal at the foot of Market Street and Sausalito on the north shore of the Bay, where the ferries were met by the narrow-gauge trains of the North Pacific Coast Rail Road. A fast vessel for her time, the *San Rafael* could make 18 knots an hour.

On the foggy evening of November 30, 1901, she was rammed by the ferryboat, *Sausalito,* and sank off Alcatraz Island with the loss of three lives.

This incident has been recorded for history in the opening of Jack London's novel *The Sea Wolf.* 59

The San Francisco Bay Ferry SAN RAFAEL, 1877

Yachts, 1890: Schooner, Steam Launch, Sloop,

Yachts in the Gay Nineties were the most ephemeral of all vessels designed by naval architects. Vast sums of money were spent by rich owners competing with rivals for the fastest or most impressive vessel afloat. The decorations below decks seem gaudy today but the fashions of that day did not affect the long graceful lines or subtle proportions 60 of the ships themselves.

Steam Yacht, Cutter, and Catboat

The larger vessels were manned, skippered, and raced by paid hands. Usually the owner and his guests were the afterguard and they missed the joy of conning and working the ship themselves. There were a fair number of Corinthian, or amateur, sailors in the smaller yachts who sailed and raced without paid crews. These skippers started the trend toward the great nonprofessional sport of yachting today.

61

The Bark SHENANDOAH, 1890

The four-masted bark *Shenandoah* was one of the biggest of the Bath (Maine) Down-Easters. She represents one of the last of the big sailing vessels built of wood, and she was so highly thought of that her picture is engraved on United States Master's license certificates.

From the earliest colonial days until just before World War II, schooners were plying the coastal waters of America. As the type evolved they became larger and more graceful. They could be worked with small crews, since the heavy hauling was done with small steam donkey engines or small gasoline-driven winches.

62

The Schooner SAVANNAH, 1901

The West Coast Barkentine ECHO, 1901

The barkentine represents a compromise between the square rig for long runs before the wind and the fore and aft rig for windward work. The expense and complications of square-sail rigging are lessened by setting square sails only on the foremast and thus also reducing the size of the crew needed to man the ship.

Gloucester schooners were the culmination of the long development in sailing vessels used for fishing. They were fast, able craft, well suited to the work of banks fishing in all weather. The few survivors of this fine breed of ships are now auxiliaries with cut-down rigs.

63

Gloucester Schooners, 1902

The Battleship U.S.S. OREGON, 1898

When the Spanish American War broke out in 1898 there were fears that the Spanish fleet might bombard the cities of the eastern seaboard. The fleet of Spain was larger than that of the United States, although we had bigger and more heavily gunned vessels. In order to guard these cities, all sorts of old warships were resurrected, while our newest and best ships of the Atlantic battle fleet were detailed to seek out and destroy the Spanish fleet.

The *Oregon,* one of our newest and most powerful battleships, was sent from Bremerton, Washington, to join the Atlantic battle fleet. She sailed from Puget Sound down the Pacific Coast around South America via the Strait of Magellan and up to Florida in 68 days, averaging 11.6 knots. Never had a battleship gone so far so fast. After coaling at Jupiter Inlet, Florida, she helped defeat the fleet of Spanish Admiral Cervera at the battle of Santiago off Cuba.

In spite of the *Oregon*'s fast passage and our success at Santiago, it was strongly felt that a canal should be dug through the Isthmus of Panama to avoid the expense of a two-ocean navy. The *Oregon* like most ships combined the old and new in her design. Her ram bow was taken from the rams of ancient Greek war vessels, her fighting tops from the sailing-ship era, and her revolving turrets from the *Monitor* of Civil War fame.

The U.S.S. KATAHDIN

Ever since the time of ancient Greece, ramming another ship to sink her was considered good naval tactics. Today we know that such tactics are ineffectual particularly against fast-moving ships with adequate fire power. The turtle-like *Katahdin* was heavily built with rounded decks and reinforced bow to ram and sink hostile ships. Fortunately she never saw action — she would have been too slow to ram most of the vessels of her time.

The U.S.S. CONCORD

The gunboat *Concord,* one of Admiral Dewey's victorious squadron at Manila Bay, was considered fast for her time and well armed with six six-inch guns. She and vessels of her class were used as commerce raiders and scouts. Her three-masted schooner rig was for steadying purposes or for possible engine breakdown.

The rakish three-funneled *Dupont,* below, was a high-speed torpedo boat designed and built by Nathanael G. Herreshoff, the famous yacht designer. She carried the news of the destruction of the Spanish fleet from Cuba to America. Her engines were so beautifully built that she ran for twenty years without major repairs.

65

The U.S.S. DUPONT

Harbor Tugboat

Without the utilitarian tugboat, marine activity in the harbors of America would almost cease. Tugs help to dock big ships, tow barges and ships, and act as auxiliary fire boats in emergencies. In order to do their job they need great power; hence they are packed with 66 machinery.

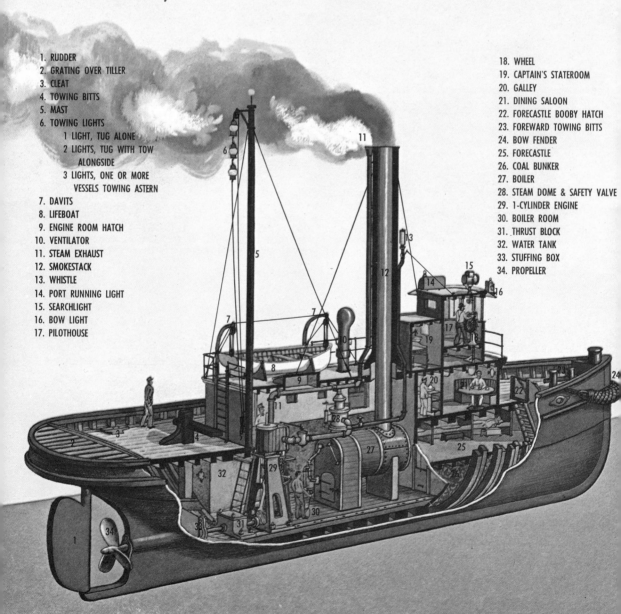

1. RUDDER
2. GRATING OVER TILLER
3. CLEAT
4. TOWING BITTS
5. MAST
6. TOWING LIGHTS
    1 LIGHT, TUG ALONE
    2 LIGHTS, TUG WITH TOW ALONGSIDE
    3 LIGHTS, ONE OR MORE VESSELS TOWING ASTERN
7. DAVITS
8. LIFEBOAT
9. ENGINE ROOM HATCH
10. VENTILATOR
11. STEAM EXHAUST
12. SMOKESTACK
13. WHISTLE
14. PORT RUNNING LIGHT
15. SEARCHLIGHT
16. BOW LIGHT
17. PILOTHOUSE

18. WHEEL
19. CAPTAIN'S STATEROOM
20. GALLEY
21. DINING SALOON
22. FORECASTLE BOOBY HATCH
23. FOREWARD TOWING BITTS
24. BOW FENDER
25. FORECASTLE
26. COAL BUNKER
27. BOILER
28. STEAM DOME & SAFETY VALVE
29. 1-CYLINDER ENGINE
30. BOILER ROOM
31. THRUST BLOCK
32. WATER TANK
33. STUFFING BOX
34. PROPELLER

The S.S. MAURETANIA

The most beautiful and successful of the foreign transatlantic liners that sailed between the United States and Europe was the British four-stacker *Mauretania*, built in 1906. A perfect picture of grace and utility, she held the Atlantic Blue Ribbon as the fastest ship in trans-atlantic shipping for twenty-two years. With her quadruple screws she steamed at 27 knots, her regular service speed.

Neither fast nor graceful were the tramp cargo steamers. Bluff-bowed, plain, and rugged, these vessels carried cargo from port to port performing the useful tasks that keep the wheels of industry turning. 67

A Tramp Cargo Ship, 1912

The Battleships U.S.S. FLORIDA and U.S.S. UTAH, World War I

Until World War II the major fighting ship of all navies was the battleship, the direct descendant of the ship of the line of the sailing-ship era (see illustration, page 25). Its function was to slug it out with hostile battleships in line of battle. All the other ships in the fleet were designed to protect, aid, or inform the battleship of the enemy's whereabouts. A battleship's armament consisted of 10- or 12- or 14-inch guns in twin turrets and from 15 to 20 lighter guns. All the vital parts of the ship were heavily armored. The heaviest protection being in a 12-inch-thick belt of solid steel amidships. As an indication of its ability to take punishment the German battleship *Seydlitz* sustained 21 direct hits from high-explosive armor-piercing shells at the battle of Jutland, 1916, and remained afloat.

During World War I our navy did not engage in any major big-ship battles. The mere threat of the overwhelming power of the combined British and United States naval forces kept the German fleet bottled up at Kiel after we belatedly came into the conflict. Most of our naval activities consisted of convoy work and submarine chasing, both highly important, dangerous and necessary tasks.

By 1915 the destroyer had become a very important American naval unit. Affectionately nicknamed "tin cans" by their crews, destroyers were narrow, very fast (32 knots), jammed with machinery, and notorious for their pitching and rolling. During the war they saw important service on anti-submarine patrol, convoy and fleet duty.

Destroyer

The 110-foot wooden, gasoline-engined submarine chasers were dubbed the "splinter fleet." Their armament consisted of a one-inch gun forward, a machine gun on top of the pilot house, and, at the stern, a Y gun that threw the barrel-like depth charges clear of the ship when attacking a submarine. Eighteen of these ships crossed the Atlantic to help clear the Mediterranean Sea of enemy submarines.

Submarine Chaser

Many of our merchant ships and quite a few of our warships were sunk by German submarines during this war. All the warring nations had submarines, but the Germans used them with such ruthless efficiency against Allied shipping that they came close to winning the war.

Submarine

Mine sweepers, frequently converted trawlers, bore the dangerous task of sweeping the seas clear of enemy mines. Two sweepers towed a cable equipped with cutting devices that detached the mines from their anchors and allowed them to come to the surface, where they were blown up by rifle fire. 69

Mine Sweeper

Great Lakes Bulk Freighter

After World War I, the need for bigger ships on the Great Lakes was felt because of the expansion of heavy industry throughout the area. As a result, some of the least graceful but the most functional ships in the world became the Great Lakes cargo ships. They are vast steel boxes pointed at the bow, rounded at the stern, having the engines aft. They are capable of carrying tremendous loads of cargo, some of the largest as much as 20,000 tons. During the ice-free months of the year, they plow through the Great Lakes from Duluth to Buffalo, moving enormous quantities of ore, grain, and coal, or a deckload of automobiles.

The Lakes passenger ship is the inland ocean liner. It has all the comforts of the ocean-going variety plus the advantages of slight rolling and many stops at ports along the way.

Great Lakes Passenger Ship

Diesel-powered Triple-screw River Towboat

Supplanting the romantic wooden, steam-driven, stern-wheel river towboats (see page 58) these highly efficient Diesel-powered, steel, screw-propeller vessels push as many as 12 barges, each holding enough cargo to fill 50 railroad cars. These powerful ships work their way from Pittsburgh to New Orleans and up to St. Paul, making our inland waterways vital arteries of commerce.

The crews of these vessels work very hard, for the tow has to be broken up at the entrance to each lock and reassembled at the exit. They are compensated by good wages, comfortable quarters, and incomparably good food.

71

The U.S.S. NORTH CAROLINA, World War II

A 45,000-ton battleship steaming ahead at 30 knots, bristling with big guns full of life and menace, was a never-to-be-forgotten sight. These vessels were the backbone of our fleet. Great floating fortresses nearly 900 feet long, firing nine 16-inch radar-aimed guns with a range in excess of 20 miles, they carried 148 antiaircraft guns ranging from 5-inch to 20-millimeters. Two thousand men, mostly highly trained specialists, were needed to man one of these giants.

During World War II battleships performed many useful tasks. They reduced shore fortifications, covered amphibious landings, and fought in many battles. But it was found that these most powerful of war vessels could be helpless unless used in conjunction with a balanced naval force of both ships and airplanes. Air cover has become an absolute necessity in naval engagements today.

It was inevitable that the aircraft carrier was to replace the battleship as the major capital warship in the fleet. We have seen that the carrier changed sea warfare as much as any development in naval history. These ships with destroyer, cruiser, and battleship escorts have become the balanced task force. In World War II, the carriers bore the brunt of the fighting. The attack on Pearl Harbor was launched from Japanese carriers. The defeat of the Japanese task force at Midway islands was chiefly a carrier victory. The battle of Leyte Gulf was fought by balanced naval forces featuring the flattops with their aircraft.

Today's carriers are a far cry from the converted collier the *Langley,* America's first experimental carrier of 1927. The biggest displace 45,000 tons and launch swarms of jet aircraft, many capable of carrying the atom bomb. They are protected by armor plate and antiaircraft weapons of all sizes. The masts and superstructures are dotted with radar equipment for fire control and for spotting airplanes and ships. Their tremendous size pemits them to store unusually large supplies of plane fuel, ammunition, torpedoes, and bombs.   73

The U.S.S. ENTERPRISE and Destroyer, World War II

Submarine

Under the pressure and urgency of wartime, many new types of ships are developed and old types improved. Utility and function are the only criterion, hence some of these vessels are rather odd-looking compared to earlier, more graceful types.

Submarines were equipped with a snorkel or breathing tube enabling them to run submerged for longer periods of time.

Many of these vessels were designed 74 for mass production and many PT's,

Patrol Torpedo Boat, PT

Landing Craft Vehicle and Personnel, LCVP

Landing Ship Tank, LST

Corvette

LST's, LCVP's, and LCT's were built and launched on the Great Lakes and the inland river ports. They were sent under their own power or towed to the sea and thence to the war zones.

Rockets designed for better accuracy and reliability could be launched in barrages from special vessels. The amphibious "duck" is a unique vessel. It has a propeller and rudder like a motorboat's, plus wheels that enable it to come to a beach, roll up to dry land, and operate as a truck.

75

Landing Craft Tank, LCT

Rocket-launching Craft

Amphibious Truck, DUKW ("Duck")

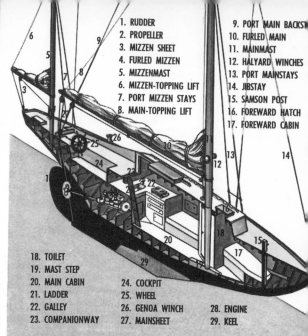

1. RUDDER
2. PROPELLER
3. MIZZEN SHEET
4. FURLED MIZZEN
5. MIZZENMAST
6. MIZZEN-TOPPING LIFT
7. PORT MIZZEN STAYS
8. MAIN-TOPPING LIFT

9. PORT MAIN BACKSTAY
10. FURLED MAIN
11. MAINMAST
12. HALYARD WINCHES
13. PORT MAINSTAYS
14. JIBSTAY
15. SAMSON POST
16. FOREWARD HATCH
17. FOREWARD CABIN

18. TOILET
19. MAST STEP
20. MAIN CABIN
21. LADDER
22. GALLEY
23. COMPANIONWAY

24. COCKPIT
25. WHEEL
26. GENOA WINCH
27. MAINSHEET

28. ENGINE
29. KEEL

38-foot Wooden Cruising Yawl

Many changes have taken place in the yachting scene since 1890. The very large yachts have vanished. The sport has become more amateur in the best sense. The number of people on the water has increased by leaps and bounds, most of them running their own boats and enjoying doing so. The amateur skipper and crew who win a Bermuda race are not only a very proud lot but highly skilled.

New materials are being used in boatbuilding today. There are plywood and Fiberglas plastic hulls, Dacron and nylon sails, nylon ropes,

30-foot Fiberglas Racing Sloop

1. RUDDER
2. STANDING BACKSTAY
3. MAINSHEET
4. FURLED MAINSAIL
5. SPREADERS
6. MAST STAYS

7. JIBSTAY
8. MOORING CLEAT
9. FLOTATION COMPARTMENTS
10. ALUMINUM MAST
    HALYARDS INSIDE IT

11. MAST STEP
    HALYARDS BELAY TO IT
12. SHELTER CABIN
13. COCKPIT

14. GENOA WINCH
15. TILLER
16. LEAD KEEL

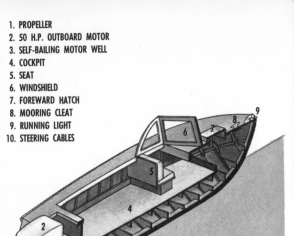

1. PROPELLER
2. 50 H.P. OUTBOARD MOTOR
3. SELF-BAILING MOTOR WELL
4. COCKPIT
5. SEAT
6. WINDSHIELD
7. FOREWARD HATCH
8. MOORING CLEAT
9. RUNNING LIGHT
10. STEERING CABLES

16-foot Plywood Outboard Runabout

aluminum masts and spars, and stainless-steel rigging. New techniques in transportation by trailer are making it possible for fairly large sail and outboard boats. to be taken to distant bodies of water for sailing, cruising, and fishing. Boatels are springing up on the water so that small boats can tie up and the owners rent rooms in them as they do in motels. For the outboarders there are marine service centers where motors are oiled, greased, and washed. Here, too, the boats can be hoisted out of the water and stored under cover in a marine garage. 77

35-foot Wooden Motor Cruiser

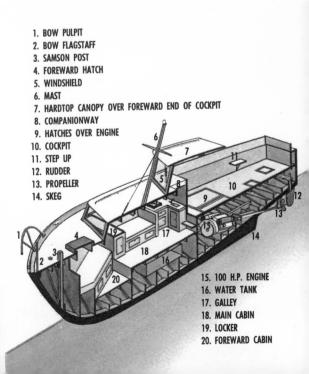

1. BOW PULPIT
2. BOW FLAGSTAFF
3. SAMSON POST
4. FOREWARD HATCH
5. WINDSHIELD
6. MAST
7. HARDTOP CANOPY OVER FOREWARD END OF COCKPIT
8. COMPANIONWAY
9. HATCHES OVER ENGINE
10. COCKPIT
11. STEP UP
12. RUDDER
13. PROPELLER
14. SKEG
15. 100 H.P. ENGINE
16. WATER TANK
17. GALLEY
18. MAIN CABIN
19. LOCKER
20. FOREWARD CABIN

Fire Boat and Ocean Liner

Today New York Harbor is an even more bustling place than it was in 1717 (pages 20–21) and 1850 (pages 48–49). The only sails seen today are on yachts passing through. The harbor is so full of traffic that yachts usually go under auxiliary power for a vessel under sail only is at the mercy of wind and tide and runs the risk of collision.

Ships have become bigger and bigger, for a big ship can carry more passengers or cargo for less per tonnage mile than a small one. Whenever possible a mechanical device has replaced the toil of men or

78

Oil Tanker and Fishing Boat

Floating Grain Elevator and Ferry Boat

animals. For example, in the past grain was carried in sacks on men's backs into the holds of ships. Today the odd-looking, floating-tower grain elevator known as an "Irish Battleship" because the crews are all men of Irish descent, loads and unloads grain pneumatically with great speed. Instead of going to Staten Island in a Whitehall boat, being rowed in a calm, or sailed in a breeze, we ride a powerful turbine-driven ferry guided by radar in fog and steam-heated for comfort in winter.   79

Train Barge, Tug, and Cargo Ship

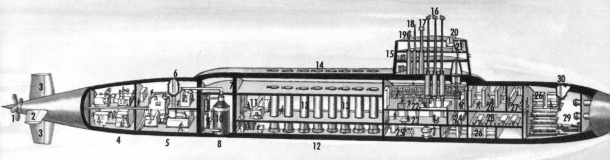

1. PROPELLER	8. REACTOR COMPARTMENT	16. PERISCOPES	24. OFFICERS' DINING ROOM
2. DIVING PLANE	9. REACTOR	17. SNORKEL	25. GYROSCOPE COMPARTMENT
3. RUDDER	10. BOILER	18. RADIO ANTENNA	26. ENLISTED MEN'S QUARTERS
4. AFT ENGINE ROOM	11. MISSILE-LAUNCHING MACHINERY	19. RADAR	27. ENLISTED MEN'S HEAD
5. FOREWARD ENGINE ROOM	12. MISSILE COMPARTMENT	20. OUTER BRIDGE	28. ENLISTED MEN'S DINING ROOM AND GALL
6. ENGINE ROOM ESCAPE HATCH	13. MISSILE TUBES	21. INNER BRIDGE	29. TORPEDO COMPARTMENT
7. SHIELDING	14. OUTER MISSILE HATCHES	22. CONTROL COMPARTMENT	30. FOREWARD ESCAPE HATCH
	15. SAIL (CONNING TOWER)	23. OFFICERS' LOUNGE AND STATEROOMS	

Cutaway of a Polaris Missile-launching Nuclear Submarine

Capable of running at full speed submerged for 100,000 miles, the atomic submarine is the newest marine marvel. Jules Verne dreamed of such a vessel one hundred years ago. Today atomic power is the spectacular driving force for our newest subsurface craft.

During World War I submarines were known as "pigboats." Space was limited, the vessel was a maze of pipes, tanks, and machinery. After being submerged for a long while the air became foul. Hence the nickname. The undersea vessels of today are a different matter entirely. The air the men breathe is so pure that when the ship surfaces the crews complain the air smells fishy. The power delivered to the propeller is so smooth that the sensation when submerged is like sitting in your own living room. In contrast to earlier submersibles, the atomic submarine is faster when submerged than on the surface. Living quarters are still not roomy on today's submarines — the ships are jammed with machinery and weapons — but compared to the earlier vessels they are marvels of comfort.

The fact that these vessels can remain submerged for weeks on end makes the selection of men for the crew most important. They must be of calm temperament, yet quick and active mentally and physically. Recruiting for the submarine service is all on a voluntary basis. Food and all the amenities are the best the navy can provide for all hands

and the cook.

The tremendous power of the atom is being used today to propel surface ships as well as undersea craft. The vessel shown here is capable of sailing 350,000 miles at 20 knots. A vessel of the same size propelled by conventional Diesel or steam engines can cover about 13,000 miles at the same speed before a refueling stop.

The cargo-carrying capacity of the atomic ship is only slightly larger than that of a conventional ship because what is gained by not having to carry fuel is offset by the great weight of the shield around the atomic pile.

The cost of a ship driven by nuclear fission is about twice that of a ship driven by ordinary power. But the savings in time and fuel will partially compensate for the greater initial cost.

The men who go down to the sea in ships today have every modern convenience for navigation safety and comfort that engineering skill and technology can devise, but they still know and respect the sea as their forefathers did — it can be a treacherous element, and a good sailor is ever on the alert. It is to the credit and valor of these men that America continues to sail the seas. 81

The Nuclear Ship SAVANNAH

INDEX AND GLOSSARY

Barkentine

Bark

83

Brig

Brigantine—A two-masted vessel, brig-rigged except for a fore-and-aft mainsail, *20, 24*

Brigantine

Briggs, Enos, 40
Brooklyn, side-wheel river steamer, *47*
Browne, Charles, 37
Buck—To go against tide or river current, 58
Bugeye ketch—A two-masted, ketch-rigged, shallow-draft, double-ended vessel found on Chesapeake Bay.

Bugeye Ketch

Bulk carrier—A ship designed to carry heavy, loose cargo, 45
Buoys—Cans, cones or spars set in navigable channels, 12

Cable—Anchor line, 41
Canoes: bullboat, 3, *3;* Chippewa, 5, *5;* dugout, 3, *3* (Chesapeake, 3, *3;* Haida, 4, *4;* Seminole, 3, *3*); Hudson's Bay, 5, *5;* Penobscot, 5, *5*
Caravel—A three- or four-masted vessel having square sails on the foremast and lateen sails on the other masts.

Caravel

Careen—To tip a vessel to one side for repairs, *13, 40,* 41
Cargo ship, *67, 79*
Carronades. *See* Guns
Cat ketch—A two-masted vessel having the mainmast at the extreme bow.

Cat Ketch

Cat schooner—A two-masted vessel having the foremast at the extreme bow; a schooner without bowsprit or headsail.

Cat Schooner

Catboat—A fore-and-aft-rigged vessel having the single mast at the extreme bow, *21, 61*

Catboat

Centerboard—A board or plate in a centerline watertight slot which when lowered prevents leeway, 48

Champlain, Lake, battle of, 22, 23

Chandlery, ship—The store of a dealer in ships' supplies, 21

Chart—A marine map, 11, 12, 16

Chebec—A three-masted, lateen-rigged vessel, *33*

Chebec

Cherub, H.M.S., 41, *41*

Christiaensen, Hendrick, 16

Civil War ships, 52, 53, *53*, 54, *54*, 55, *55*, 56, *56*, 57, *57*

Cleopatra, 46, *46*

Clermont. See Steamboats

Clipper ship, 50, *50*, 51, *51*

Coaling—Filling a ship's bunkers with coal, 64

Columbus, Christopher, 8, 9, 10, 11

Concord, U.S.S., 65, *65*

Confederate ships. *See* Civil War ships

Conning—Guiding a vessel, 61

Constellation, a Great Lakes steamer, *45*

Constitution, U.S.S., 32, *32*, 33, 38, *38*, 40

Convoy, 27, 68, 69

Coppers—Copper tanks over the galley stove in which cooking was done, 43

Corvette—An anti-submarine escort vessel, 75

Crews: clipper ship, 51; of Columbus' ships, 8, 9, 10; dining saloon, 66, *80;* gun, 31, *31;* helmsmen, *10, 19, 66;* life at sea in 1812, 42, 43; *Mayflower*, 17, 18, 19; quarters (crew), *19, 30, 30,* 43, *55, 55, 66, 66,* 80, *80;* quarters (officers), *19, 42, 42, 55, 66, 66, 80;* submarine, *80;* toilet facilities, *42, 43, 76, 80;* river boat, 35; tugboat, 66; Viking ship, 7; warship, 43; yacht, 61

Cruiser, 73; motor, 77, *77;* yawl, 76, *76*

Cutter—A single-masted fore-and-aft-rigged vessel having the mast a third of the length from the bow, *22, 24, 24, 61*

Cutter

Cutter, square-topsail—A cutter carrying a square topsail, *22, 23*

Square-topsail Cutter

85

Dauphine, 12, *12*
Depth charge, 69
Derby's Wharf, *34*
D'Estaing. *See* Estaing, Count Charles d'
Destroyer, 69, *69*, 73
Detroit, H.M.S., *36*
Diesel power, river towboat with, *71*
Discovery, 14, *14*
Dory—A flat-bottomed, seaworthy rowboat pointed at the bow; the stern has a narrow triangular transom, *63*, 78

Dory

Draft—The depth at which a vessel lies in the water, 47, 48, 54, 58
Drake, Edwin L., 44
Drake, Sir Francis, 13
Drakkar, 6, *6*, 7, *7*

Drakkar

Draw. *See* Draft
Driving, hard—Sailing a ship to the limit of its capabilities, 51
Duck. *See* Amphibious truck
Dupont, U.S.S., 65, *65*

Echo, a barkentine, 63, *63*
Engine, atomic: submarine, 80, *80;* of the *Savannah*, 81
Engines, gasoline: motor cruiser, 77, *77;* outboard runabout, 77, *77;* sub chaser, 69; cruising yawl, 76, *76*

Engines, steam: Boulton and Watt, 37, *37; Clermont's*, 37, *37; Dupont's*, 65; Evans', 36, *36;* Fitch's, 36, *36;* of Long Island Sound steamer, 46, *46; Monitor's*, 55, *55;* of river steamer, 47; Rumsey's, 36, *36;* Stevens', 36, *36;* tugboat, 66; *Virginia's*, 54; walking beam, 46, *46*
Enterprise, U.S.S., 73
Ericsson, John, 55
Ericsson, Lief, 6
Essex, U.S.S., title page, 40, *40*, 41, *41*
Estaing, Count Charles d', 25
Evans, Oliver, 36
Experiment, H.M.S., 27, *27*

Felucca—A single-masted, double-ended, lateen-rigged fishing boat found on San Francisco Bay, 59

Felucca

Ferry boat, 59, *59*, 79, *79*
Fiberglas or plastic, 76
Fire boat, 66, 78
Fire control, 73
Fire power, 23
Fishing vessels, 11, *11*, 63, *63*, 78
Fitch, John, 36
Flatboat, 35, *35*
Floors—The area at the bottom of a ship between the keel and the turn of the bilge, 51
Florida, U.S.S., 68
Food and drink: on Columbus' ships, 8, 9; dining saloons, *43*, 66, 80; galley, 17, 18, 19, *19*, 26, 29, 55, *55*, 66, *66*, 76, *76*, 77, *77*, 80, *80;* Pilgrims', 17; fourgon, 10; on Long Island Sound steamer,

46; on river boats, 35, 71; on submarines, 80; on United States ships in 1812, 43; Vikings', 7; water tank, 77

Fore—Toward the bow or front of a ship.

Fore-and-aft-rigged—Having sails set in line with the keel (*see* Sloop *and* Schooner), *16, 20, 21, 22, 23, 24, 48, 49, 60, 61, 62, 63, 65, 76, 78*

Foremast hands—Ordinary sailors, so designated because they lived in the forecastle forward of the foremast, 42

Fortyn, a Dutch bark, *16*

Founder—To fill with water and sink, 13

Four-stacker—A steamer having four smoke pipes, *67, 69*

Fourgon. *See* Food and drink

Freeboard—The section of a ship between the waterline and the gunwale.

Frigate—A square-rigged war vessel ranging in length from 130 to 175 feet, 25, *26, 27, 27, 32, 32, 40, 40, 41, 53*

Frontenac, a side-wheel Canadian lake steamer, *45*

Fulton, Robert, 37

Galleon—A large vessel having three or more masts; 15th to 17th century Spanish or Portuguese.

Galleon

Galley—A lateen-rigged vessel, *22*

Gloucester schooner. *See* Schooner

Godspeed, a bark, *14*

Golden Hind. See *Pelican*

Gondola—A one-masted vessel with square sails, *22*

Grain elevator, floating, 79, *79*

Great Lakes cargo ship, 70, *70*

Great Lakes passenger ship, 70, *70*

Guerrière, H.M.S., 38, *38*

Gun turret, 54, *54,* 55, *55,* 64, *64,* 68, *68, 72, 72*

Gunboat, 53, 65, *65*

Gundalow—A single-masted, double-ended vessel found on the Piscataqua River, having one leeboard and a lateen sail.

Gundalow

Gunnery, 38

Guns: antiaircraft, 72, 73; breech loader, *10;* carronades, 31, *31, 38,* 40, 41; Dahlgren, 55, *55,* 56, *56;* Falconet, *10;* long, 31, *31;* machine, 69; nine-inch, 54; one-inch, 69; seven-inch rifled, 54; six-inch, 65; sixteen-inch radar-aimed, 72; ten-, twelve-, and fourteen-inch, 68; Y, 69

Hackett, R. J., 45

Half Moon, a bark, *15*

Hermaphrodite brig—A two-masted vessel, square-rigged on the foremast and fore-and-aft-rigged on the mainmast, *52*

Hemaphrodite Brig

87

Herreshoff, Nathanael G., 65
Hornet, U.S.S., 40
Hudson, Henry, 15, 16, 20
Hull, cutaways and external features of: clipper ships, 51, *51;* cruisers (motor), 77, *77;* of the *Mayflower*, 17, 18, *18,* 19, *19;* of the *Monitor*, 55, *55;* of the *Raleigh*, *26;* runabouts (outboard), 77, *77,* of the *Santa Maria*, 8, 9, 10, *10;* ship of 1800, *30;* ship of 1812, 42, *42,* 43, *43;* ship under construction, *29;* sloop, 76, *76;* submarine, 80, *80;* tugboat, 66, *66;* Viking ship, 6, *6;* yawl, 76, *76*
Hull, Isaac, 38
Humphreys, Joshua, 32

Inland waterways—The system of canals, locks, lakes, and rivers in the Mississippi watershed, 71
"Irish battleship," 79, *79*
Iron Age, a stern-wheel towboat, 58, *58*
Ironclad—A war vessel sheathed with iron plates, 53, 54, *54*

Katahdin, U.S.S., 65, *65*
Kearsarge, U.S.S., 57, *57*
Keelboat—A freight boat, 35, *35*
Ketch—A two-masted vessel in which the mizzenmast is placed just forward of the rudder post, *20*

Ketch,

Kit. *See* Mess kit
Knot—A unit of speed equivalent to one nautical mile per hour; one knot equals 1⅛ land miles per hour, 54, 59, 69, 72

Lake Erie, battle of, 39, *39*
Landing Craft Tank, LCT, 75, *75*
Landing Craft Vehicle and Personnel, LCVP, *74,* 75
Landing Ship Tank, LST, *74,* 75
Langley, U.S.S., 73
L'Antonio, hermaphrodite brig, *52*
Lateen—A triangular sail extended by a long yard at an angle of 45 degrees to the mast.
Lateen galley—A two-masted lateen-rigged vessel that could be rowed or sailed, *22*

Galley

Lawrence, U.S.S., 39, *39*
Lexington, U.S.S., 24, *24*
Lighter, harbor. *See* Scow
Lock—A boxlike structure with gates at each end enabling vessels to pass from one level to another in a canal, 71
Longboat—The largest and strongest boat belonging to a vessel, 17, *18, 19*
Lug rig—A square sail fastened to a yard at the top, having no boom.

Lug Rig

Mauretania, British ocean liner, 67, *67*

Mayflower, a bark, 17, *17,* 18, *18,* 19, *19*

Merrimac, U.S.S., burned, rebuilt, and converted to the C.S.S. ironclad *Virginia,* 53, 54, *54*

Mess kit, or kid—A round or oval wooden tub in which food was served, 43

Mine—An anchored, submerged container filled with explosives set to blow up on contact, 69

Mine sweeper, 69, *69*

Mississippi, U.S.S., 53

Mississippi River steamer, 47, *47,* 58, *58,* 71, *71*

Mobile Bay, battle of, 56

Monitor, U.S., 54, *54,* 55, *55;* battle between the *Merrimac* and, 54

Motor cruiser, 77, *77*

Motor torpedo boat (PT), 74, *74*

Muzzle-loading gun—One that loads through the front end, or muzzle, rather than through its rear end, or breech, 31, *31, 55, 56*

New York Harbor: in 1717, 20, *20,* 21, *21;* in 1850, 48, *48,* 49, *49;* today, 78, *78,* 79, *79*

Newport, Christopher, 14

Niagara, U.S.S., 39

Niña, a bark, 9, *9*

Nocton, a British packet ship, 40

North Carolina, U.S.S., 72

Nuclear power, 80, 81

Nuclear ship, *81*

Nuclear submarine, *80*

Ocean liners: *America* (today), 78; *Mauretania* (1906), 67, *67;* side-wheel (1851), *49*

Officer country—The section of a ship where the officers eat and sleep, 42, *42*

Oil tanker, *78*

Onrust, a sloop, 16, *16*

Oregon, U.S.S., 64, *64*

Outboard guardrails. *See* Sponsons

Outboard motor. *See* Engines, gasoline

Packet ship—A fast mail and passenger ship running on a regular schedule, 40, *48*

Paddle wheel—A wheel having projecting boards or buckets for propelling a vessel, *36*

Paddle-wheel steamer. *See* Steamboats

Patrol Torpedo Boat, PT, 74, *74*

Pelican, a bark, 13, *13*

Periagua—A workboat.

Periagua

Perry, Oliver Hazard, 30

Pheobe, H.M.S., 41, *41*

Pigboat—A submarine, 80

Pilot schooner. *See* Schooner

Pinkey schooner. *See* Schooner

Pinta, a bark, 9, *9*

Port—The left side of the ship looking forward.

Porter, David, 40, 41

Preble, Edward, 33

President, U.S.S., 32

Privateer—A vessel owned and officered by private persons but engaging in maritime war with government license, 24, 34

Prize crew—A crew put aboard a captured vessel by its capturer, 40

Propeller, 36, *55,* 66, *75,* 76, *77,* 80

PT. *See* Patrol Torpedo Boat, PT

Queen of Clippers, ship, *50*

Raft: tule, 3, *3;* log, 35, *35*

Rake—To fire along the length of a vessel.

Raleigh, U.S.S., 26, 27, *27*

Ram—To run into a hostile vessel, sinking or damaging her by means of a sharp, reinforced projection at the bow of the ramming vessel, *56, 56, 64, 65, 65*

Rifled—Having a spirally grooved bore or barrel.

Rigging: of the *Mayflower, 18, 19;* of the *Raleigh, 26;* of the *Santa Maria, 10;* of ship of 1800, *30;* of sloop (racing), *76;* of United States ship of 1812, *42, 43;* of yawl (cruising), *76*

River steamers, Mississippi. *See* Mississippi River steamer

R. J. Hackett, 45

Rocket-launching craft, *75*

Rudder—A broad, flat device hinged vertically at the stern of a vessel to direct its course, *6, 10, 18, 19, 26, 29, 42, 51, 55, 55, 66, 76, 77, 80*

Sails: of Columbus' ships, *8;* of the *Mayflower, 18;* of ship of 1800, *30;* of ship of 1812, *42;* of sloop, *76;* of Viking ship, *6, 6;* of yawl, *76*

Salem, Mass., *34, 40*

San Rafael, San Francisco Bay ferry, *59, 59*

Santa Maria, Columbus' flagship, *8, 8, 9, 10*

Sausalito, San Francisco Bay ferry, *59*

Savannah, an atomic ship, *81, 81*

Savannah, a four-masted schooner, *62, 62*

Schooner—A fore-and-aft-rigged vessel having two or more masts.
Cat. *See* Catboat
Gloucester, *63, 63*

Indian Header

Indian header—A vessel with a long curved stem that sweeps down from the bowsprit to the keel, *63*

Schooner—continued

Knockabout—A vessel on which the bow is elongated, eliminating the bowsprit, *63, 63*

Knockabout Schooner

Pilot—A fast, seaworthy vessel developed for cruising in all weathers around the entrances of ports for the purpose of taking pilots to incoming ships and taking them off outgoing vessels, *48, 49, 49*

Pinkey—A double-ended vessel with an extended overhanging stern.

Pinkey Schooner

Square-topsail—A vessel having square topsails on the fore and mainmasts, *22, 23*

Square-topsail Schooner

Schooner—continued

Staysail—A vessel having a triangular staysail and fisherman's staysail instead of a gaff-headed foresail.

Staysail Schooner

Two-masted, 48, 49, *49*, 60, 63, *63*
Three masts or more, 45, 62, *62*, 65, *65*

Three-masted Schooner

Scow—A large flat-bottomed boat, lighter or barge, *20, 35, 36, 36*
Screw. *See* Propeller
Seydlitz, an Imperial German Navy ship, 68
Shallop—A heavy boat with one or more masts.
Shenandoah, a four-masted bark, 62, *62*
Ship—Strictly speaking, a ship is a three-

Ship

masted (or more) vessel which is square-rigged on all masts, *21, 25, 26, 27, 32, 34, 40, 41, 44, 48, 50*
Ship of the line—A ship large enough to be in the line of battle, 25, *25*, 53, *53*
Ship sloop—A small ship-rigged warship with guns on the upper deck only, 53
Shipbuilding, 28, *28*, 29
Shipbuilding tools. *See* Tools, shipbuilding
Shoal—An area where the water is shallow.
Side wheel—A paddle wheel placed on each side of a vessel.
Slaver, 52, *52*
Sloop—A one-masted fore-and-aft-rigged vessel, 48, *48*, 60, 76, *76*
Gaff sloop ill.

Gaff Sloop

Hudson River sloop, 48, *48*
Marconi sloop ill.

Marconi Sloop

Racing sloop, 76, *76*
Sloop of war. *See* Ship sloop

Sloop—continued

Square-topsail sloop—A sloop carrying a square topsail, *21*

Square-topsail Sloop

Smooth-bore gun—A gun having a barrel that is not grooved or rifled.

Snow—A brig-rigged vessel having a small mast close to the main lower mast and parallel to it upon which the small fore-and-aft mainsail is set.

Snow

Sponsons—Triangular platforms placed before and abaft of a paddle wheel.

Sprit rig—A one- or two-masted, small, fore-and-aft-rigged vessel, having the peak of its sail extended by a spar or sprit, *16, 20, 21*

Sprit Rig

Square sail—A quadrilateral sail extended by a yard normally at right angles to the keel.

Square-rigger—A vessel whose principal sails are square.

Starboard—The right side of a ship looking forward.

Stern—The rear part of a ship.

Stern wheel—The paddle wheel placed at the rear of a vessel.

Yawl

JOHN O'HARA COSGRAVE II

John O'Hara Cosgrave was born in San Francisco and spent his boyhood sailing an old whaleboat, called the *Moby Dick,* up and down San Francisco Bay and its tributaries. In fact his love of sailing so far outdistanced his love of school that though he later graduated to a ketch named the *Typee* that he rebuilt himself, he had greater trouble graduating from the various schools that he attended in the Bay area.

Following a junior year at the University of California as an art major — A-minus average that year! — he went to Paris for two years of study (with the painter André Lhote) and travel, and has made his living as an artist ever since.

During the war he was attached to the Office of Strategic Services where he illustrated instruction books on such recondite subjects as how to blow up trains, sink ships, and otherwise add to the discomfort of the enemy.

Mr. Cosgrave has done book jackets and illustrations for nearly all of the better-known American publishers and his work has appeared in many magazines, including *Fortune, Life,* and *Yachting.* He is best known for his marine watercolors of American ships and shipping.

America Sails the Seas was ten years in the making, and in addition to the actual writing and painting represents countless hours of research in museums all over the world, among them the Science Museum and the Greenwich Museum in London, the Musée de la Marine in Paris, the Musée Naval in Toulon, and the Musée de Marine et d'Outre-Mer in Marseilles. Here in the U.S. he continued his research in the Museum of the City of New York, the New-York Historical Society, the Watercraft Collection at the Smithsonian Institution, Washington, D.C., the Peabody Museum in Salem, Massachusetts, and in the marine museums in Nantucket and New Bedford, Massachusetts, Mystic, Connecticut, and San Francisco.

Mr. Cosgrave worked on the book during the wintertime in his house in Brooklyn, New York, and in summers at his modern beach house on Cape Cod, where the book had to compete with the pleasure of sailing a Herreshoff bull's eye sloop.